ALOYSIUS J. COPPERTHWAITE.

AD CAPTANDUM VULGUS

COPPERTHWAITE AGED 6 MONTHS

THE COPPERTHWAITE FAMILY CREST.

COPPERTHWAITE AGED 17¾ YEARS.

The Copperthwaite Research Team's
Special Thanks
go to

Mr Derek Copperthwaite
of Ripley's Believe-It-or-Not Museums, USA
who started the whole Copperthwaite trail.

The late Mr Ed Millborrow
who created the first Copperthwaite Retrospective Exhibition
and to BBC Television News who adopted the show.

Ms Jacky Cowdrey
of the Records Room, Royal Albert Hall, London
for her research efforts into the Steam-Powered Orchestra
and for her generous offer of a concert in the Hall's kitchen.

Mr Frank Muir
for his interest and encouragement in the Copperthwaite Project:
'I do congratulate you on bringing the work of Copperthwaite to a
wider public.'

Mrs Alexandra Wedgwood
The Architectural Archivist, Record Office, House of Lords,
London, for her interest
and willingness to place the Copperthwaite 'National Lion Clock'
papers in the
Architectural Archive in the Victoria Tower.

Lt Col R G Dalton, BSc (Eng)
Bridge Master, Tower Bridge London for his confirmation of the
esteem in which
'The Prof' is still remembered in the Bridge environs and for his
account of yet another invention (not recorded in the
Scrapbooks) of 'a device to prevent loose material created by
the Bridge's horse traffic falling from the rising bascules'.

Dr David Bellamy
for his encouragement for the Scrapbook and his welcome
comment when spirits were at a low
ebb and the publishing deadline close at hand – a 'fabulous project'.

Miss Pamela Clark
Assistant Registrar, Royal Archives, Round Tower, Windsor Castle
for her assistance in checking the Royal Archives for references
to the inflatable marquee at Buckingham Palace.

Mr Frank Atkinson
Librarian, St Paul's Cathedral for braving the elements to check
on the current status of St Paul's Dome and for confirming the
entries in the Verger's (R R Green) diary for 16th August 1861.

Mr K P J West
General Manager and Licensee of The Blackpool Tower
for his time checking the Tower Archives for further information
on Copperthwaite's Candle Factory.

Mr W D F Grant
Area Civil Engineer of ScotRail for his assistance in the
research on the Forth Bridge Whisky Distillery and his official
confirmation that 'there are no unexplained holes or fittings on
the Bridge nor is any part oak lined'.

Mr Stephen Jobbs
President of Apple Computers, California, USA who provided the
Mackintosh computers
which made the exhaustive research into the Copperthwaite
material a simpler task.

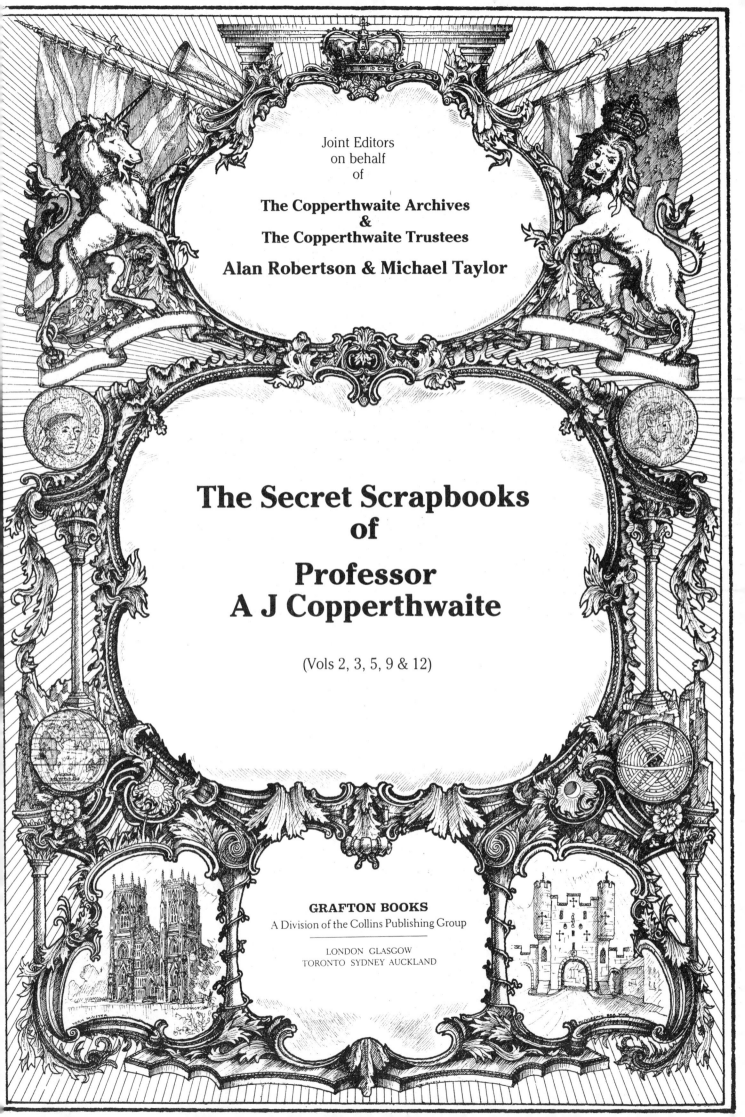

Joint Editors
on behalf
of

**The Copperthwaite Archives
&
The Copperthwaite Trustees**

Alan Robertson & Michael Taylor

The Secret Scrapbooks
of

Professor
A J Copperthwaite

(Vols 2, 3, 5, 9 & 12)

GRAFTON BOOKS

A Division of the Collins Publishing Group

LONDON GLASGOW
TORONTO SYDNEY AUCKLAND

The Editors
would like to thank
the following specialists for their assistance
in the preparation of the Copperthwaite Scrapbooks:

Betty Taylor
for endless cups of tea, coffee and her excellent fruitcake during times of
stress and panic when research kept meeting brick walls and numerous
blind alleys.

Michael Fong
for long hours in the dark room restoring
the Copperthwaite photographic glass plates
and achieving excellent silver bromide prints.

Bill Cook
for his dedicated restoration of the Wentletrap Model

Kevin Benson
for his restoration of the
Tower Bridge Boat-Wash Model

Christopher Howes
for his work on the
Nelson's Columbrella Model

James Merryweather
for his unique assistance with the
Copperthwaite project

Grafton Books
A Division of the Collins Publishing Group
8 Grafton Street, London W1X 3LA

A Grafton Paperback Original 1986

Copyright © Optimum Design Ltd

ISBN 0-586-07043-5

Printed and bound by Scotprint.

Professor A J Copperthwaite's MOST IMPORTANT ARCHITECTURAL IMPROVEMENTS

The
COPPERTHWAITE CHRONOLOGY
Being a summary of the
MORE IMPORTANT ARCHITECTURAL IMPROVEMENTS
conceived by Professor A J Copperthwaite abstracted from the Copperthwaite Scrapbooks
Volumes 2, 3, 5, 9 and 12 and the AJC Diaries
for the years 1834-1900.

Additional sources include:-

The British Architectural Society
The Architectural Review and Journal
The London Central Records Office
Punch
Feathered Fancier
The British Conchology Journal
Herpetological Digest and Informer
Proceedings of the Welsh Office
The Herbalist
The Yorkshire Horologist

Scottish Civil Engineer
The Trough or Gentleman's Caterer
The Brunel Research Society
Lloyds Shipping Gazette
Hansard
The Pondkeeper & Fancy Fish Fanatic
Catering Circular
Trinity House Report
The Chanter

and many other sources — see bibliography and research sources.

1835-1837	Glastonbury Torrey & Herbal Gardens
1852-1854	Crystal Palace All-London Laundry & Public Baths
1858-1860	Stonehenge National Early Warning Defence System
1859-1864	Albert Hall Fully Automatic Steam-Powered Orchestra
1866-1867	Buckingham Palace Inflatable State Marquee & Automatic Guard Changing Device
1870-1873	Nelson's Columbrella
1873-1874	The Furry Trout Trap (construction phase)
1875-1877	Caernarvon Castle Carp Farm & Aquarium
1876-1879	Brighton Pier Cross-Channel Dirigiplane Terminal
1879-1880	The Wentletrap — A Gentleman's Shell Dredging Vessel
1880-1881	Tower of London Rotating Restaurant & Aviary
1885-1887	Sphinx Solar-Powered 'I Speak Your Weight' Machine
1881-1883	St Michael's Mount Partially Floating Telescope (incomplete records — not included in this edition)
1883-1884	Edinburgh Castle Soundproof Bagpipe Training School (incomplete records — not included in this edition)
1887-1888	Eddystone Lighthouse Wave-Powered Fishing Machine (incomplete records — not included in this edition)
1890-1893	Forth Railway Bridge Whisky Store & Distillery
1896-1898	Tower Bridge Sail-Through Boatwash
1897-1900	Blackpool Tower Candle Manufactory
1900-1902	St Paul's Cathedral Rota-Dome
1906-	Big Ben National Clock

A contemporary portrait miniature from The National Miniature Gallery — Copperthwaite's Tower Bridge Boatwash can just be distinguished in the background.

A J Copperthwaite . . . .
Architect and Visionary
Born 1812 – Died 1913

Known affectionately as 'The Artless Architect' by his companions, Professor A J Copperthwaite has always been, and remains to this day, one of the great enigmas and unforgettable characters of the nineteenth century.

His voluminous diaries and scrapbooks record that his working life was devoted to 'making monuments more animate'. Despite these reasonable and worthy ambitions, all too few of his designs survive to the present day in their original form.

Like all visionaries, many of his inventions and improvements were greeted with scepticism; some with outright scorn and derision, some just with hostility.

Sir Edwin Lutyens is said to have made himself ill with laughter when shown Copperthwaite's plans to turn the Sphinx into a Speak Your Weight machine 'to confound the many members of the English aristocracy who travelled to Egypt to gaze on the pyramids and poke about in the sand'.

The Church of England establishment was an enthusiastic supporter of his alternative design for St Paul's Cathedral, in which the dome was rotated at great speed by wind power in order to activate the organ bellows. The obvious economic benefits of this scheme were lost in the later clerical condemnation of his use of Bishops' mitres to act as revolving incense burners on the dome.

But like all great eccentrics he battled against the establishment, seeking always to bring the Empire to the forefront of scientific achievement and international acclaim. His more notable designs included all aspects of 'improvement' from public laundries; castellated carp farms; rotating restaurants to giant floating telescopes. In every endeavour he carried his basic ideas and concepts through all levels of the scheme down to the minutiae of clothing design, power sources and the effect on the environment and the natural world.

Not all his designs were totally serious – many show an admirable sense of humour frequently lacking in the Victorian era. Many may even look slightly ridiculous to modern eyes but all are based firmly in scientific principles and engineering practices and have stood the test of time – except perhaps his work on the Forth Railway Bridge.

Today, these Scrapbooks, gathered together for the first time since they were compiled, will, hopefully, set the record straight on a unique and highly original Yorkshireman. Perhaps the naive and honest, frequently reactionary, qualities of his work will be better appreciated, and establish A J Copperthwaite on a par with Christopher Wren, John Vanburgh and Arthur ffrench-Getty as a creator of genuine architectural art, and establish him in his true niche – as a true British genius.

The silver Trafalgar Trophy presented by the Trafalgar Square Residents Association to the best Furling Horse.

Professor Aloysius J Copperthwaite

WILLIAM SMITH.
1715 ~ 1773.
ECCENTRIC YORKSHIRE FARMER; THE FIRST MAN IN BRITAIN TO ATTEMPT TO BREED THE HEDGEHOG FOR ITS MEAT. RENOWNED FOR HIS ABILITY TO GROW THE BEST MELONS IN BRITAIN.

ANDREW SMITH.
1754 ~ 1809.
TOOK OVER HIS FATHERS FARM ON THE YORKSHIRE COAST IN 1773. HE BECAME A VERY POPULAR SMUGGLER, BUT WAS EVENTUALLY CAUGHT WITH THIRTY BARRELS OF RUM HIDDEN IN HIS MIDDEN.

JOSHUA SMITH.
1755 ~ 1814.
A HARD WORKING AND WELL RESPECTED MAN IN WHITBY, JOSHUA BUILT HIS REPUTATION, AND HIS VAST FORTUNE, ON HAVING THE CLEANEST COLLIER BRIGS IN BRITAIN. IN HIS WILL HE LEFT £100,000.

THOS. ANDREW SMITH.
1786 ~ 18 ?
A STRANGE, INDEPENDENT MAN DEVOTED, SO HE CLAIMED, TO HELPING THE POOR. HE WAS PARTICULARLY INTERESTED IN FALLEN WOMEN. THIS LED TO HIS ARREST IN 1821. HIS FATE IS NOT RECORDED.

MURIEL RUNDSWICK.
1735 ~ 1786.
DAUGHTER OF THE OWNER OF A SMALL TRAVELLING CIRCUS IN YORKSHIRE. SHE BECAME FAMOUS THROUGHOUT THE COUNTY FOR HER ABILITY TO JUGGLE MELONS WITHOUT USING HER HANDS.

DAVID SMITH.
175·? ~ 1802.
RESPECTED CITIZEN OF YORK, AND THE MANUFACTURER OF THE FINEST BOOTS AND SADDLES IN THE COUNTY. HIS FAVOURITE CLAIM WAS THAT HE HAD ONCE 'BOOTED' KING GEORGE III.

THE COPPERTHWAITE FAMILY.

WITH RELATIVES AND ANCESTORS OF

A.J. COPPERTHWAITE.

ARCHITECT AND VISIONARY.

1812 ~ 1913.

AMANDA SMITH.
? ~ ?
FOR THE FIRST TWENTY OR THIRTY YEARS OF HER LIFE, AMANDA WAS A HAPPY CAREFREE GIRL. THEN IN 1801 OR THEREABOUTS, SHE HAD A MEETING WITH A WELSH BARBER, AND SHORTLY AFTER THAT SHE BECAME A NUN.

CAPT. SAML. COOK.
1731 ~ 1791.
BRITISH NAVAL CAPTAIN: ALMOST DISCOVERED THE NORTH-WEST PASSAGE, BUT DUE TO HEAVY RAIN AND A BAD HEADACHE, HE DECIDED NOT TO GO. HE DISCOVERED THE SOURCE OF THE THAMES IN 1760, INSTEAD.

JOHN R. COOK.
176·? ~ 1830?
LIKE HIS FATHER, JOHN WENT TO SEA AS A YOUNG CABIN BOY, AND BY THE 1790'S HE HAD COMMAND OF HIS OWN SHIP. HE VANISHED DURING A VOYAGE ROUND THE WORLD AND IS THOUGHT TO HAVE 'GONE NATIVE' IN HAWAII.

ULRIKA DUCHKOVA.
1742 ~ 1784.
CZECHOSLOVAKIAN, DAUGHTER OF DIMITRI, A MERCHANT. ULRIKA WAS REPUTEDLY THE MODEL FOR THE FIGURE-HEADS OF AT LEAST TWELVE NAVAL FRIGATES AND ONE BOMB KETCH IN EUROPE.

ANASTASIA COOK.
1766 ~ ?
A QUIET, SOLEMN WOMAN, ANASTASIA HAD AN UNDYING PASSION FOR TAPESTRY. SHE DESIGNED A TWO HUNDRED FOOT LONG TAPESTRY OF THE SPANISH INQUISITION.

MARIA COOK.
1765 ~ 1854.
HOUSEKEEPER TO MANY MEMBERS OF THE GENTRY AND FAMILIES OF HIGH REPUTE IN YORKSHIRE AND NOTTINGHAMSHIRE, ALSO A LADY OF STRIKING BEAUTY. SHE CLAIMED TO HAVE TAUGHT MRS. BEETON ALL SHE KNEW."

EMILY SMITH.
1788 ~ 1870.
AN EXCESSIVELY SHY LADY, EMILY REFUSED TO HAVE HER PORTRAIT PAINTED FROM THE FRONT, AND INSISTED THE ARTIST WAS TO WORK FROM THE HOUSE OPPOSITE, USING A TELESCOPE. THIS IS THE ONLY PORTRAIT OF HER.

THOMAS COPPER~THWAYTE. 1710~1753.
CARPENTER AND ARTIST, GAINED CONSIDERABLE WEALTH MAKING JEWEL-STUDDED WARDROBES FOR THE ARISTOCRACY.

JOHN H. COPPER~THWAITE. 1737~1810.
A RATHER DOUR MAN, BUT KIND HEARTED. HE MADE A CONSIDERABLE FORTUNE MANUFACTURING FARM MACHINERY.

ALOYTIOUS J. COPPER~THWAITE. 1812~1913.
ALOYTIOUS INHERITED FROM HIS FATHER ENOUGH MONEY AND PROPERTY TO ELIMINATE THE NEED TO WORK DURING HIS LIFE. HE WAS FREE TO DO EXACTLY WHAT HE WANTED TO...

JUSTINE HENDRIK. 1718~1760.
JUSTINE WAS A HAPPY, NOISY AND GOOD-NATURED DUTCH WOMAN, WHOSE VOICE, IT WAS CLAIMED, OFTEN SAVED VESSELS FROM SHIPWRECK ON THE FOGY YORKSHIRE COAST. SHE DIED CHOKING ON AN OYSTER.

JUSTINE COPPER~THWAYTE. 1739~1792.
ALTHOUGH A LADY OF PLEASING LOOKS, SHARP WIT AND PLEASANT PERSONALITY, JUSTINE REMAINED A SPINSTER ALL HER LIFE.

SAMUEL BRIDLINGTON COPPER~THWAITE. 1776~1829.
A MAN OF SEVERE DISCIPLINE AND QUICK TEMPER, BUT HONEST AND JUST. INHERITING HIS FATHER'S AGRICULTURAL MACHINERY BUSINESS, HE BUILT IT UP AND EXPANDED IT, PRODUCING VARIOUS VEHICLES AND GOODS IN HIS MANY FACTORIES. HE HAD A PASSION FOR FACTORIES, AND WOULD BUILD A NEW ONE ON THE SLIGHTEST EXCUSE. HE BUILT TWO IN BRADFORD SIMPLY BECAUSE HE LIKED THE MAYOR. IF HE COULDN'T FIND WORKERS OR MACHINERY, HE WOULD PAY MEN TO STAND IN THE EMPTY BUILDINGS AND 'MAKE MECHANICAL NOISES' WHEN HE VISITED THE PLACE. HIS ONE DISAPPOINTMENT WAS THAT ALOYTIOUS WOULDN'T ENTER THE BUSINESS.

HENRIETTA COPPER~THWAITE. 1817~1885.
HENRIETTA WAS A POWERFUL WOMAN WHO INHERITED HER FATHER'S SENSE OF DISCIPLINE. SHE RAN A SMALL GIRLS SCHOOL NEAR BATH.

JOHANNES LECARRE. 1713~1761.
A FRENCH OFFICER OF REMARKABLE AND OBSESSIVE POLITENESS. FRIENDS CLAIMED THAT IN BATTLE HE SPENT MORE TIME APOLOGISING TO THOSE HE INJURED THAN HE DID ACTUALLY INJURING THEM.

CLAUDETTE LECARRE. 1742~?
STAR OF STAGE AND MAGIC LANTERN SHOW, CLAUDETTE BECAME A GREAT CELEBRITY IN THE THEATRES OF LONDON. SHE CLAIMED THAT SHE COULD SING IN TEN DIFFERENT LANGUAGES, INCLUDING HEBREW.

SUSAN COOPER. 1715~1757.
A SHY GIRL OF SCOTTISH PARENTS, SUSAN ALWAYS WISHED TO MARRY A SOLDIER, BECAUSE, SHE CLAIMED, THEIR TIGHT UNIFORMS GAVE THEM POLITE VOICES.

LUISE LECARRE/BAUGNIET. 1740~1812.
WIDOW OF CAPT. CLAUDE BAUGNIET, LUISE WAS A RATHER FLIRTATIOUS WOMAN. HOWEVER HER SECOND MARRIAGE WAS HAPPY.

CELIA ANNE SMITH. 1784~1824.
CELIA ANNE INHERITED BOTH HER MOTHER'S BEAUTY AND HER COOKING SKILL, BUT HER GREATEST TALENT LAY IN HER ABILITY TO CREATE WORKS OF ART. IN THE BACKGROUND OF THIS PORTRAIT CAN BE SEEN HER MODEL OF A CHINESE PAGODA, CONSTRUCTED ENTIRELY FROM OLD USED THEATRE TICKETS AND ANIMAL-HOOF GLUE. SHE COULD PLAY SEVERAL MUSICAL INSTRUMENTS, INCLUDING THE PIANO, BUT BECAME THE CENTRE OF ATTENTION AT MANY PARTIES WHEN SHE PRODUCED HER CELLO, AS SOON AS HE SHOWED AN INTEREST IN ART, ALOYTIOUS BECAME HER FAVOURITE CHILD, MUCH TO HER HUSBAND SAMUEL'S ANNOYANCE. 'ART' HE CLAIMED ANGRILY, 'IS FOR WOMEN AND CHILDREN, AND HAREM EUNUCHS.'

CELIA COPPER~THWAITE. 1813~1860.
CELIA HAD A GREAT LOVE FOR ANIMALS, AND BUILT, WITH FINANCIAL AID FROM ALOYTIOUS, A HOME FOR NEGLECTED ANIMALS IN A DISUSED FACTORY.

JOSIAH COPPER~THWAITE. 1815~1874.
JOSIAH WAS SAMUEL'S FAVOURITE CHILD, AS HE SHOWED ENTHUSIASM TO TAKE OVER THE BUSINESS. SADLY, HE PROVED TO BE A POOR BUSINESSMAN.

"*What, Another?*"

Copperthwaite's Fine-Powder Custard
No Eggs!   No Trouble!   No risk

As used by Professor Copperthwaite on board his famous exploration
vessel 'The Wentletrap' in a wide variety of recipes. 'I would never be
without my Fine-Powder Custard in the roaring forties. It can be relied
upon to stay in my bowl in any weather'.

*The Professor enjoyed a 'reliable and steadfast' image with
the British public; consequently his name and image were
frequently used as endorsements for commercial products.
This contemporary advertisement for Copperthwaite's
Custard would have met with his full approval as he
enjoyed it as a regular part of his diet. He is also on record
as using the congealed remains in his architectural model-
making – which might explain why so few models have
survived to this day.*

*Previous page. A Copperthwaite Family Tree drawn by
AJC's sister Celia. She was fascinated by the family
genealogy and spent long hours researching their past.
Both had the same tutor as children and she obviously
shared the Professor's gift for penmanship and his
idiosyncratic spelling.*

CRYSTAL PALACE ALL-LONDON LAUNDRY & PUBLIC BATHS 1852-1854

After the success of the Great Exhibition in 1851 Professor Copperthwaite realised, as did many other men of vision, that a permanent use should be found for the huge glass Crystal Palace.

He approached the Palace designer, Joseph Paxton, with his scheme to 'utilise the building as a laundry and bathing house for the filthy working classes and disgusting poor of London who should all know better . . .'

This he argued, would be 'an opportunity to wipe out the filth and lice-ridden squalor of the poor, whilst given the common working man an opportunity to improve his knowledge and mind by viewing the wondrous exhibits in the concourse of the Palace as his humble raiments dried!'

As well as washing facilities for clothes, carpets and bedding there would be bathing facilities, both private and public.

From these quite humble beginnings the scheme quickly caught the imagination of the leading proponents of public welfare and the endeavour blossomed into a self-contained facility capable of catering for the cleanliness of the entire population of London. A contemporary broadsheet – with many of the illustrations produced by Copperthwaite – shows that even HM Queen Victoria gave her blessing to the operation and performed the opening ceremony – bringing a token collection of palace laundry on the Irish State Coach.

The Professor was also called upon to 'turn his mind and energies' to provide labour saving devices to assist in the total cleansing process' and many of these are illustrated in his broadsheet.

Victoria's life-long confidant, John Brown, insisted that 'the Sassenach mind be not neglected' and advocated that the 'cleansing of the mind be most encouraged'. This evidently proved somewhat difficult in practice, the pages of the Good Book becoming rather unmanageable in the Palace's damp atmosphere, and the readings were replaced by community hymn singing in the Great Hall. Brown's Scottish frugality was evident by his suggestion (in a letter to the Bath Master) that the 'still-tepid water after use in the private bathing chambers be circulated to the common ablution areas rather than simply flushed away'. Such was the rich consistency of this waste water that it was eventually collected in giant vats and transported to Kew Gardens to nourish the Royal Rhubarb.

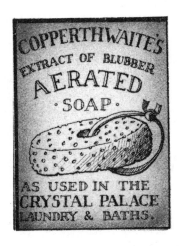

A spurious advertisement which appeared at the same time as the opening of the Crystal Palace All-London Laundry and Public Baths.

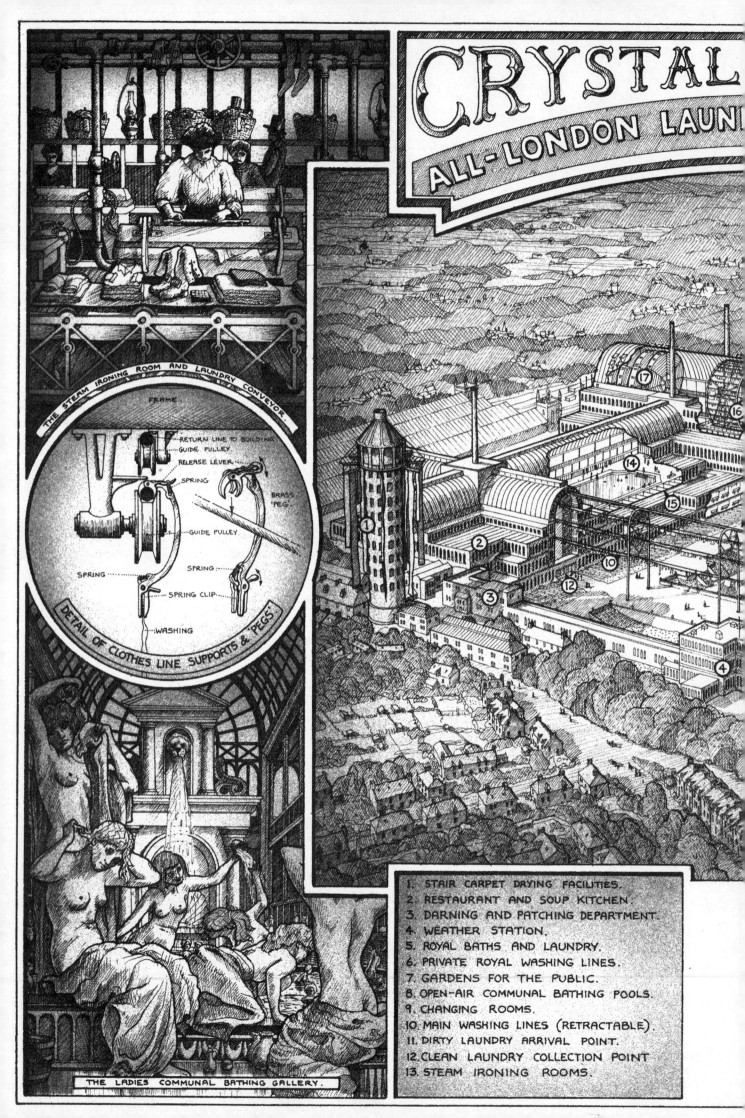

CRYSTAL
ALL-LONDON LAUNDRY

THE STEAM IRONING ROOM AND LAUNDRY CONVEYOR

DETAIL OF CLOTHES LINE SUPPORTS & 'PEGS'

FRAME

RETURN LINE TO BUILDING
GUIDE PULLEY
RELEASE LEVER
SPRING
BRASS 'PEG'
GUIDE PULLEY
SPRING
SPRING
SPRING CLIP
WASHING

THE LADIES COMMUNAL BATHING GALLERY.

1. STAIR CARPET DRYING FACILITIES.
2. RESTAURANT AND SOUP KITCHEN.
3. DARNING AND PATCHING DEPARTMENT.
4. WEATHER STATION.
5. ROYAL BATHS AND LAUNDRY.
6. PRIVATE ROYAL WASHING LINES.
7. GARDENS FOR THE PUBLIC.
8. OPEN-AIR COMMUNAL BATHING POOLS.
9. CHANGING ROOMS.
10. MAIN WASHING LINES (RETRACTABLE).
11. DIRTY LAUNDRY ARRIVAL POINT.
12. CLEAN LAUNDRY COLLECTION POINT
13. STEAM IRONING ROOMS.

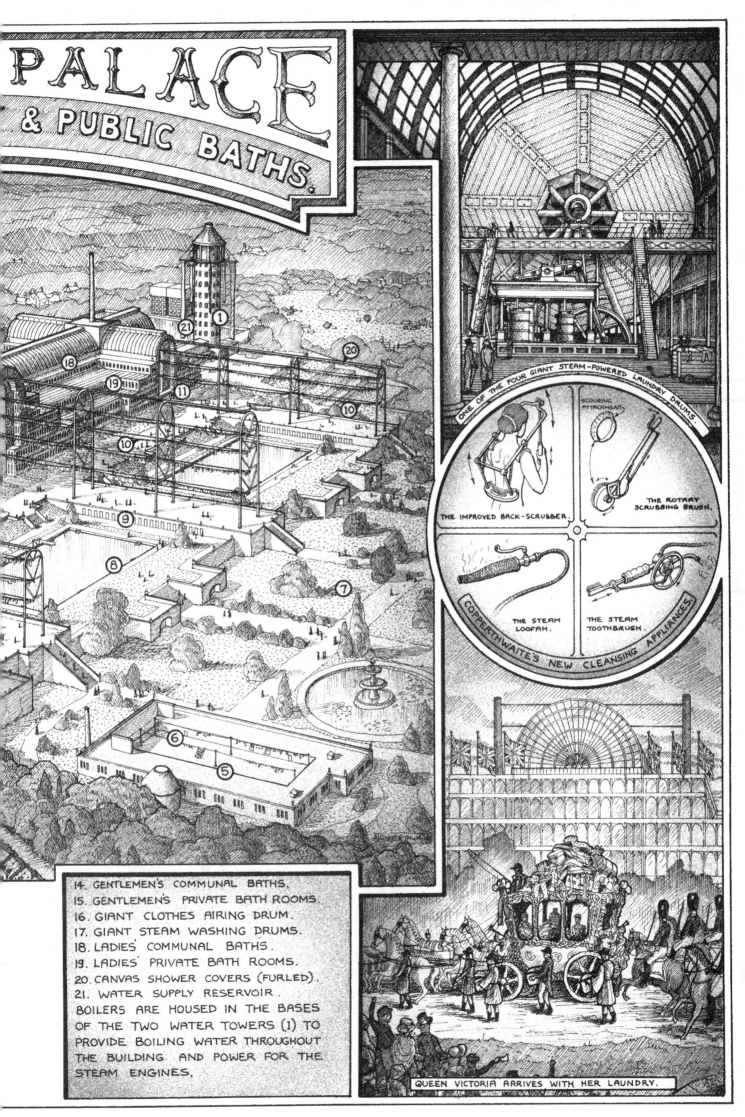

PALACE & PUBLIC BATHS.

ONE OF THE FOUR GIANT STEAM-POWERED LAUNDRY DRUMS.

THE IMPROVED BACK-SCRUBBER.

SCOURING ATTACHMENT.

THE ROTARY SCRUBBING BRUSH.

THE STEAM LOOFAH.

THE STEAM TOOTHBRUSH.

COPPERTHWAITE'S NEW CLEANSING APPLIANCES.

14. GENTLEMEN'S COMMUNAL BATHS.
15. GENTLEMEN'S PRIVATE BATH ROOMS.
16. GIANT CLOTHES AIRING DRUM.
17. GIANT STEAM WASHING DRUMS.
18. LADIES' COMMUNAL BATHS.
19. LADIES' PRIVATE BATH ROOMS.
20. CANVAS SHOWER COVERS (FURLED).
21. WATER SUPPLY RESERVOIR.
BOILERS ARE HOUSED IN THE BASES
OF THE TWO WATER TOWERS (1) TO
PROVIDE BOILING WATER THROUGHOUT
THE BUILDING AND POWER FOR THE
STEAM ENGINES.

QUEEN VICTORIA ARRIVES WITH HER LAUNDRY.

STONEHENGE NATIONAL EARLY WARNING DEFENCE SYSTEM 1858-1860

Professor Copperthwaite caused quite a stir amongst academics following his first visit to Stonehenge in 1857. He claimed to have unearthed a slab bearing symbols that proved the construction of the huge monument was an attempt by a small group of Druids to protect themselves from the warmth of their gods after they formed a trades union.

The original Druid protection device persuaded Copperthwaite that a modern system could be designed for national defence based on the ley lines radiating from the ancient monument. He produced several plans for Stonehenge, but the most complete set of drawings to survive illustrates his scheme for the very first complete early warning system. A series of catapults were to be built, protected by the restored structure of the stone circle. These catapults would form a circle, each one aimed at a second catapult approximately half a mile away. The shot from the first catapult would trigger off the second; this would trigger off a third, and so on, until the chain of shots reached a major town or city. The last shots in each triggered off a large cannon, warning the populace of attack. A huge telescope scanned the horizon from the top of the restored monument, watching for the first sign of impending invasion.

Copperthwaite's scheme had obvious merits and was well received in military circles, but a relatively hysterical editorial in The London Chronicle suggested that the populace would be in more danger from cannon balls flying wildly about in all directions above their heads than from any known enemy of the day. The Early Warning System was mothballed, much to the Professor's disgust, and was only built in miniature in his Yorkshire estate when marbles were 'shot' in place of cannon balls and the 'enemy' was invading rabbits.

A page from a sketch book dated 1858-59.

THE 1858 CAMP SITE, STONEHENGE. NECESSARY TO AVOID PEACE CAMPAIGNERS!

AJ COPPERTHWAITE.

⊓ STONEHENGE ⊓

A TRUE DESCRIPTION OF THE MONUMENT'S ORIGINAL FORM AND PURPOSE, AND DETAILS OF THE PROPOSED STONEHENGE NATIONAL 'EARLY WARNING' SYSTEM FOR NATIONAL DEFENCE.

AN IMPRESSION OF A BURST OF WRATH FROM THE GODS STRIKING THE STONEHENGE UNION SHELTER. WRATH WAS 'EARTHED' THROUGH THE VERTICAL 'ALTAR STONE'.

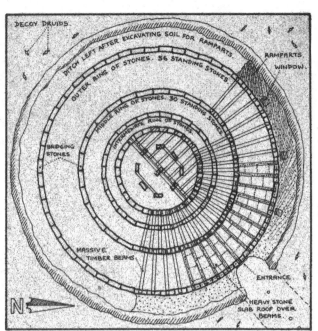

A PARTLY RESTORED PLAN OF STONEHENGE AS IT WOULD HAVE APPEARED IN 1700 BC. WHEN IT WAS BUILT. ITS ORIGINAL PURPOSE WAS TO PROTECT A GROUP OF DRUIDS FROM THE WRATH OF THE GODS WHEN THEY FORMED A TRADES UNION.

A LARGE DRUID UNION MEMBER WEARING HIS PERSONAL 'WRATH CONDUCTOR' FOR PROTECTION OUTSIDE THE STONEHENGE SHELTER. WRATH IS 'EARTHED' THROUGH THE BALL AT HIS FEET.

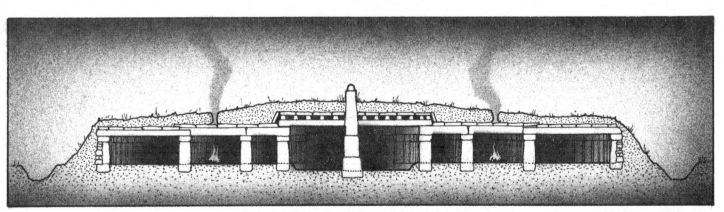

A CROSS-SECTION THROUGH THE ORIGINAL STONEHENGE UNION SHELTER, 1700 BC. THE DRUIDS SLEPT BETWEEN THE HUGE UPRIGHT STONES, FOR ADDED PROTECTION AGAINST BURSTS OF 'OVERNIGHT WRATH'.

'DECOY-DRUID' THESE WERE SET UP TO HELP CONFUSE THE GODS.

THE ORIGINAL 'COPPERTHWAITE TABLET' FOUND IN 1857 AT STONEHENGE..WHEN DECIPHERED IT REVEALED THE TRUE PURPOSE OF THE BUILDING OF STONEHENGE.

AN UNPROTECTED DRUID AFTER AN ATTACK OF WRATH FROM THE GODS.

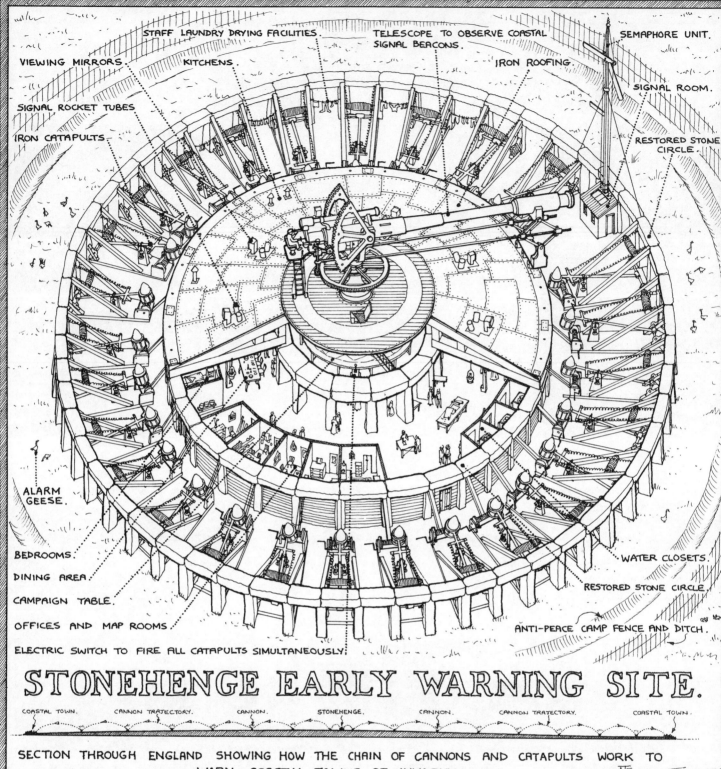

STONEHENGE EARLY WARNING SITE.

SECTION THROUGH ENGLAND SHOWING HOW THE CHAIN OF CANNONS AND CATAPULTS WORK TO WARN COASTAL TOWNS OF INVASION.

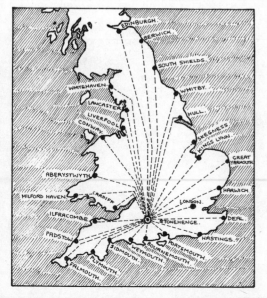

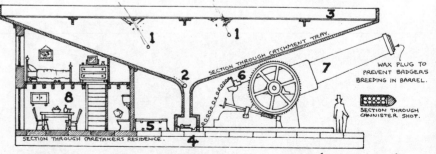

THE VELOCITY OF SHOTS FROM THE PREVIOUS CANNON (OR CATAPULT) PENETRATES THE WOOD COVERING ① (TO PREVENT STONE-THROWING CHILDREN FROM SETTING OFF THE GUN) AND ONE OF THE SHOTS FROM THE NOW EXPLODED CANNISTER ② FALLS DOWN THE CENTRE HOLE OF THE SQUARE CATCHMENT TRAY ③ AND TRIPS THE SWITCH ④. USING THE POWER FROM A BATTERY CELL ⑤ THIS FIRES THE ELECTRIC SPARK ⑥ AND SHOOTS THE GUN ⑦. THE CANNISTER FIRED REPEATS THIS PROCESS ON THE NEXT GUN. ⑧ IS THE RESIDENCE FOR THE CARETAKER.

GLASTONBURY
TORRERY & HERBAL GARDENS
1835-1837

In 1833 Copperthwaite was commissioned by the West Country Society of Druids to 'set England firmly in the centre of the known firmament' and, as an adjunct, design a landscaped farm-garden to 'develop and cultivate for the benefit of all the many rare medicinal herbs much favoured by English Druidry'.

Apart from the ancient monument at Stonehenge, Glastonbury Tor in Somerset was voted by the Druid Council to be the most magic place in England' and the Professor was invited to develop the ruins of St Michael's Church on the Tor summit.

He chose to create the Glastonbury Torrery and Herbal Gardens – happily combining his lifelong interests in Astronomy, Astrology and Homoeopathic Medicine. He constructed the world's largest and most complicated orrery actually on top of the church tower. The huge instrument incorporated all the known planets of the Solar System and revolved slowly above the re-built St Michael's powered by a clock mechanism* inside. The light from the giant illuminated Sun – which was the natural centrepiece of the revolving orrery – attracted pests and strange creatures from scores of miles around. Many of these settled in the pleasant Glastonbury atmosphere – and some thrive there still to the present day.

The surrounding Herbal Gardens were especially productive and the many rare varieties cultivated there were judged more efficacious and powerful than those grown at Kew Gardens. Copperthwaite believed that this was due to the strong magical forces attributed to the Tor and the energies generated and concentrated by the revolving Torrery. Many of the rare varieties of herbs brought to Glastonbury during this bountiful period have since been lost. The main exception is *Breathalizica tremens*, The Closing Thyme, which is still lovingly cultivated in the gardens of the 'Rat & Gooseberry' in the nearby village of Budleigh Wooton. Sprigs of this herb are still ritually distributed to local landlords every Mid-Summer's Eve and are believed to have a pacifying effect on brewery stocktakers. However, even to the present day strange foreign herbs can still be discovered flourishing in secret pockets of rich Glastonbury soil and some may well be descendants of the original Copperthwaite stock.

*A system of giant parabolic mirrors designed to capture the sun's rays and wind the clock's solar expanding bi-metal main spring was abandoned due to the inhibiting low cloud frequently found a-top the Tor.

A page from a sketch book dated 1858-59 which has some very interesting notations – the Professor had obviously run short of drawing materials and been forced to over-draw an earlier charcoal sketch of Miss Fondleton.

17

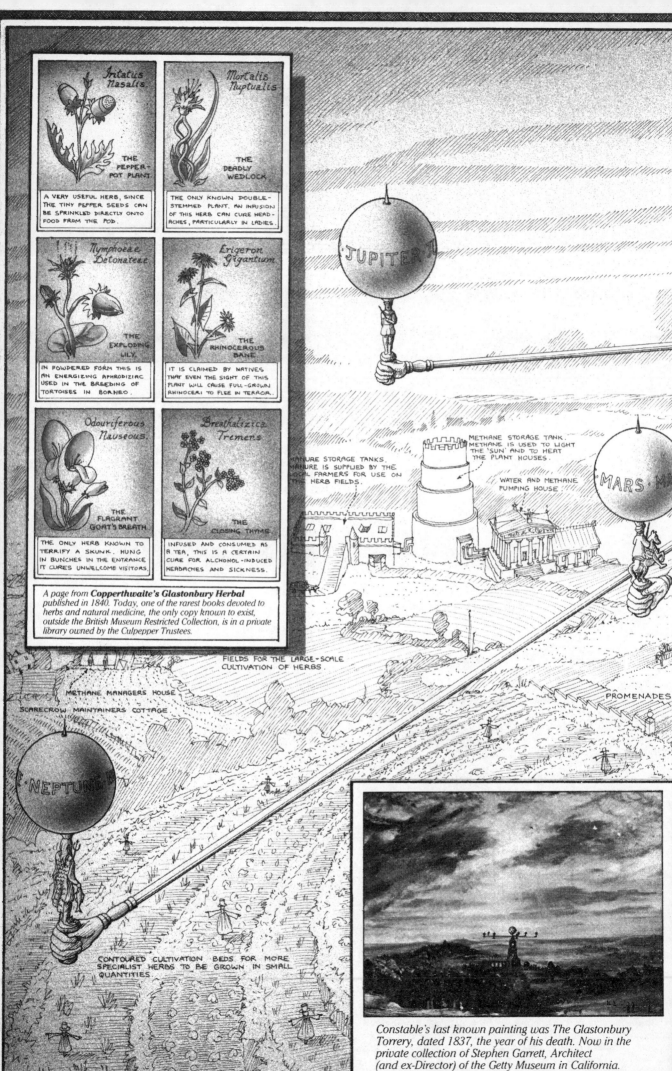

*A page from **Copperthwaite's Glastonbury Herbal** published in 1840. Today, one of the rarest books devoted to herbs and natural medicine, the only copy known to exist, outside the British Museum Restricted Collection, is in a private library owned by the Culpepper Trustees.*

Constable's last known painting was The Glastonbury Torrey, dated 1837, the year of his death. Now in the private collection of Stephen Garrett, Architect (and ex-Director) of the Getty Museum in California.

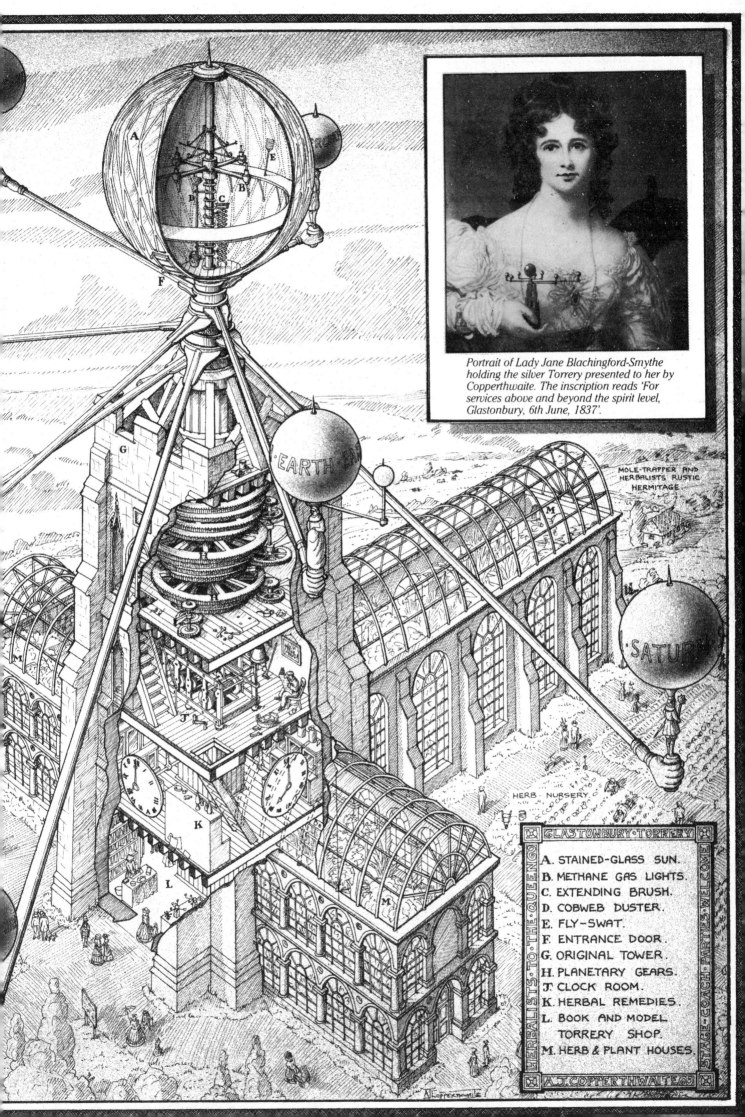

Portrait of Lady Jane Blachingford-Smythe holding the silver Torrery presented to her by Copperthwaite. The inscription reads 'For services above and beyond the spirit level, Glastonbury, 6th June, 1837'.

MOLE-TRAPPER AND HERBALISTS RUSTIC HERMITAGE

EARTH

SATURN

HERB · NURSERY

GLASTONBURY · TORRERY

A. STAINED-GLASS SUN.
B. METHANE GAS LIGHTS.
C. EXTENDING BRUSH.
D. COBWEB DUSTER.
E. FLY-SWAT.
F. ENTRANCE DOOR.
G. ORIGINAL TOWER.
H. PLANETARY GEARS.
J. CLOCK ROOM.
K. HERBAL REMEDIES.
L. BOOK AND MODEL TORRERY SHOP.
M. HERB & PLANT HOUSES.

HERBALISTS · TO · THE · QUEEN

STAGE · COACH · PARTIES · WELCOME

A.J. COPPERTHWAITE

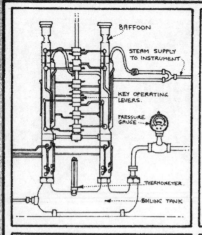

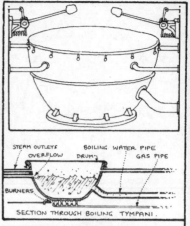

Instruments of the Steam Age:
No. 1 The Double Baffoon.
This instrument resembles a pair of Bassoons but the notes are filtered through boiling water giving them a unique fluid vibrato.

No. 2 The 120-Pound Triangle
Only steam power has the strength to hit this massive triangle and produce the full resonance of its sound.

No. 3 The Boiling Tympany
This ingenious device can eliminate the problem of drum rolls. Once struck, the action of the steam and boiling water prolongs the sound.

Craftsmen constructing the 'Animated Albert' before the figure was unveiled on the Dome. During concerts the figure would rotate, tap his right foot, and conduct — all synchronised with the Steam-Powered Orchestra.

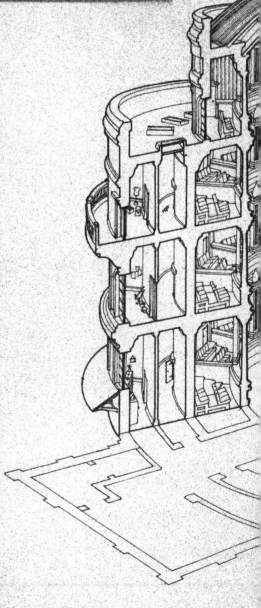

THE ALBERT HALL FULLY-AUTOMATIC STEAM POWERED ORCHESTRA.
Being a series of improvements to the existing Building by K. J. Copperthwaite. 1861.

AS THE BELT WINDS FROM ONE DRUM TO THE OTHER, THE PUNCHED HOLES ACTIVATE THE LEVERS TO PLAY THE NOTES OF THE INSTRUMENT.

SQUARED SHAFTS GUARANTEE ALL THE INSTRUMENTS ARE PLAYING TOGETHER.

The musical drum which operated the french horn in Copperthwaite's 'Concerto for Sac-But and Lancashire boiler', composed in 1861. (In B at 42 psi)

AT THE TOP OF THE BUILDING IS THE GLASS ROOM CONTAINING THE STEAM ENGINE WHICH DRIVES, THROUGH COMPLEX GEARING, THE VARIOUS MUSICAL DRUMS TO ACTIVATE THE INSTRUMENTS. STEAM FROM THE BOILER, WHICH IS HOUSED AT THE REAR OF THE BUILDING, ALSO PROVIDES THE BLOWING POWER TO THE WIND SECTION OF THE ORCHESTRA. STEAM FROM THE STEAM ENGINE IS EXPELLED THROUGH THE TWO DECORATIVE STACKS THAT FLANK THE 'ANIMATED ALBERT'

A.T.Copperthwaite.

ALBERT HALL FULLY AUTOMATIC STEAM-POWERED ORCHESTRA 1861-1867

In 1861 Professor Copperthwaite was approached by Sir Kenneth Livingstone, Chairman of the 'Bring Great Music to The Common People of London' committee, to combine the 'revolutionary power' of the steam engine with the building of the new Albert Hall.

As a frequent concertgoer (usually to the Egyptian Rooms) and orchestral enthusiast, Copperthwaite records that he was 'frequently annoyed' by the 'temperemental and unreliable nature of conductors and orchestral performers'. This annoyance led him to suggest and then design the fully automatic steam-powered orchestra for the Albert Hall. The especially commissioned music was to be punched (in the manner of the pianola) on canvas rolls. Keys activated by the holes in the canvas operated the various instruments through an ingenious series of levers and belts. Steam power operated the winding drums as well as providing the power for the wind instruments. Steam pistons operated percussion and string sections. The whole central structure was then made to revolve and musical scores totally re-written so that patrons in the surrounding boxes 'equally receive the benefits of all sections of the orchestra'.

The steam-powered automaton figure of Albert on the dome of the Tower was equipped with articulated 'conducting arms' and these motions were reflected to steam engine operatives working below by a 'camera obscura' system of prisms and mirrors. Thus the actions of the figure were always synchronised to the particular music being performed. The sound of his tapping right foot was also broadcast to the 'engine room' using a modified speaking-tube from the Royal Yacht, and controlled the musical tempo. Queen Victoria had misgivings about the use of her husband as conductor – she was evidently under the impression that he was intended to conduct lightning! Mollified by a letter of explanation from Copperthwaite, she, however, insisted that the figure of her 'beloved Albert' actually control the orchestra and not just 'reflect your excellent orchestra's endeavours'.

Local wags of the day in the coffee houses of Fleet Street joked that the 'Animated Albert' was perhaps the only time the Consort ever got 'steamed-up' about anything except Christmas trees and his beloved Great Exhibition.

For those who could not afford tickets to enter the hall, the music could be heard through large horns positioned round the building whilst the painted representation of the theme of the music travelled slowly across Kensington Gore to the Hall.

The sheet music, pierced with thousands of holes to activate the various instruments of the Steam-Powered Orchestra, passes slowly across Kensington Gore from the drum on top of the Albert Memorial. The pictorial display, always especially commissioned and painted to complement the music, adds another dimension to the event. In this example the painting illustrates 'Der Rosenkavalier' by Richard Strauss.

BUCKINGHAM PALACE INFLATABLE STATE MARQUEE & AUTOMATIC GUARD CHANGING DEVICE 1866-1867

In the 1860's Royal Garden Parties at Buckingham Palace were becoming very much a regular and prominent part of the social calendar. Extravagant fashion and flamboyant hats were the order of the day and the unreliable English weather wreaked havoc with ostrich feather and be-jewelled frock alike. Even the worthy Copperthwaite could not be expected to influence the weather and he proposed, instead, a radical solution: a suitably regal, decorative, inflatable marquee to cover the entire central courtyard of Buckingham Palace. As his scrapbook drawings illustrate, this giant waterproof canvas envelope was inflated by hot air generated in boilers powered by sewer-gas, piped underground from the London system. The outer surface of the marquee bore decorations of royal armorials and was surmounted by a giant representation of the Imperial Crown. Even in this singular feature, the Copperthwaite genius for inventiveness and foresight was not neglected – the jewels around the crown's rim were represented by polished metal mirrors which served the double purpose of warning low flying balloonists of imminent danger.

The entire structure was moored around the lower edge to special cleats on the Palace roof and could be lowered and packed away in a remarkably short time. The Sovereign's Battalion, The Military College, Sandhurst, 1866, held (and still hold) the record for deflation and stowing away in three hours, fourteen minutes following a State Reception for the Nawab of Jaipur.

Whilst the Professor was engaged on the design and construction of the Inflatable Royal Marquee, he was approached by the Commander of the Queen's Guard who requested that he look at the plight of the common Guardsman. The problem was shrinking busbies (and subsequent headaches) caused mainly by marching out to change the guard during heavy rain storms. Copperthwaite devised an automatic clock-operated guard changing device which unobtrusively raised the new guard out of site. To retain a sense of occasion a steam organ played Rule Britannia and God Save The Queen as the guard changed. The steam engine operating the organ also provided some degree of warmth for the guard on duty.

Inspired by a recent visit to Venice and the clock in the Piazza del Marco, Copperthwaite suggested that the growing number of tourists visiting London anxious to catch a glimpse of the Royal Family could be satisfied by installing life-size mechanical figures representing members of the Family, past and present, slowly moved round in procession on the Palace balcony. This suggestion was evidently not received with any real enthusiasm in the Royal Mews.

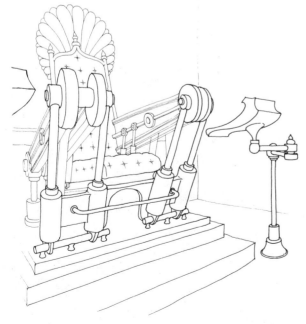

The Control Throne at the nerve centre of the sewer gas system for the raising of the Marquee.

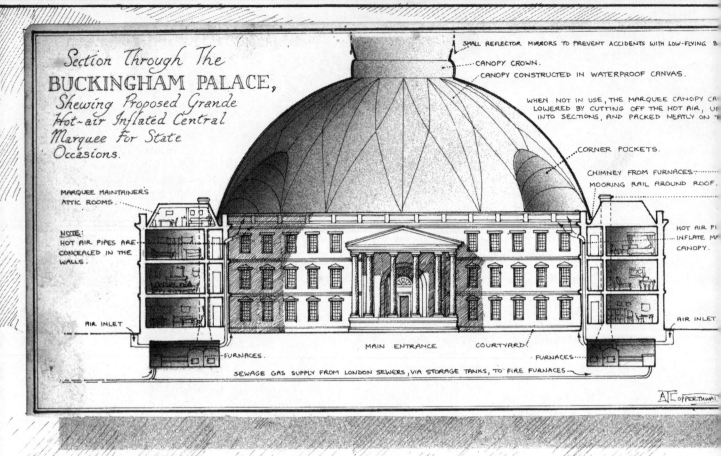

Section Through The
BUCKINGHAM PALACE,
Shewing Proposed Grande
Hot-air Inflated Central
Marquee For State
Occasions.

SMALL REFLECTOR MIRRORS TO PREVENT ACCIDENTS WITH LOW-FLYING B

CANOPY CROWN.

CANOPY CONSTRUCTED IN WATERPROOF CANVAS.

WHEN NOT IN USE, THE MARQUEE CANOPY CA
LOWERED BY CUTTING OFF THE HOT AIR, U
INTO SECTIONS, AND PACKED NEATLY ON T

CORNER POCKETS.

CHIMNEY FROM FURNACES

MOORING RAIL AROUND ROOF.

MARQUEE MAINTAINER'S
ATTIC ROOMS.

NOTE:
HOT AIR PIPES ARE
CONCEALED IN THE
WALLS.

HOT AIR PI
INFLATE M
CANOPY.

AIR INLET

AIR INLET

FURNACES.

MAIN ENTRANCE   COURTYARD

FURNACES

SEWAGE GAS SUPPLY FROM LONDON SEWERS, VIA STORAGE TANKS, TO FIRE FURNACES

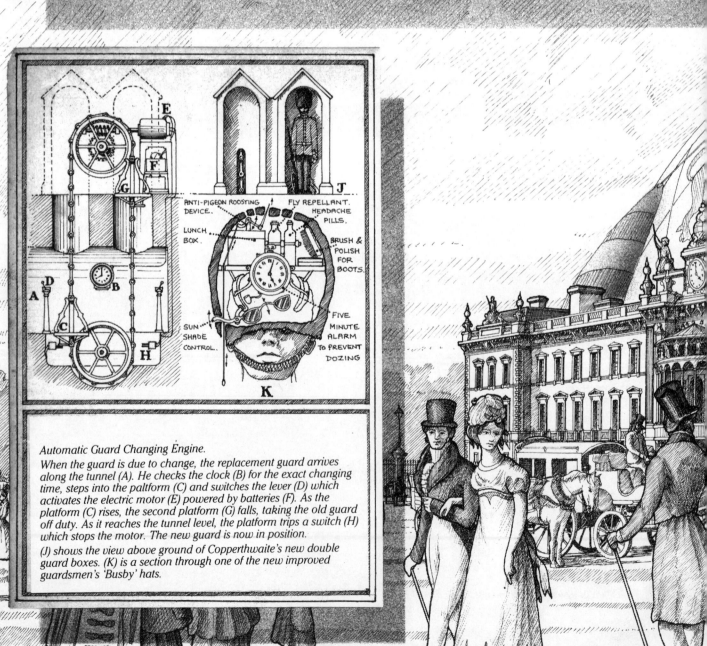

ANTI-PIGEON ROOSTING
DEVICE.

FLY REPELLANT.
HEADACHE
PILLS.

LUNCH
BOX.

BRUSH &
POLISH
FOR
BOOTS.

SUN
SHADE
CONTROL.

FIVE
MINUTE
ALARM
TO PREVENT
DOZING

Automatic Guard Changing Engine.
When the guard is due to change, the replacement guard arrives
along the tunnel (A). He checks the clock (B) for the exact changing
time, steps into the paltform (C) and switches the lever (D) which
activates the electric motor (E) powered by batteries (F). As the
platform (C) rises, the second platform (G) falls, taking the old guard
off duty. As it reaches the tunnel level, the platform trips a switch (H)
which stops the motor. The new guard is now in position.

(J) shows the view above ground of Copperthwaite's new double
guard boxes. (K) is a section through one of the new improved
guardsmen's 'Busby' hats.

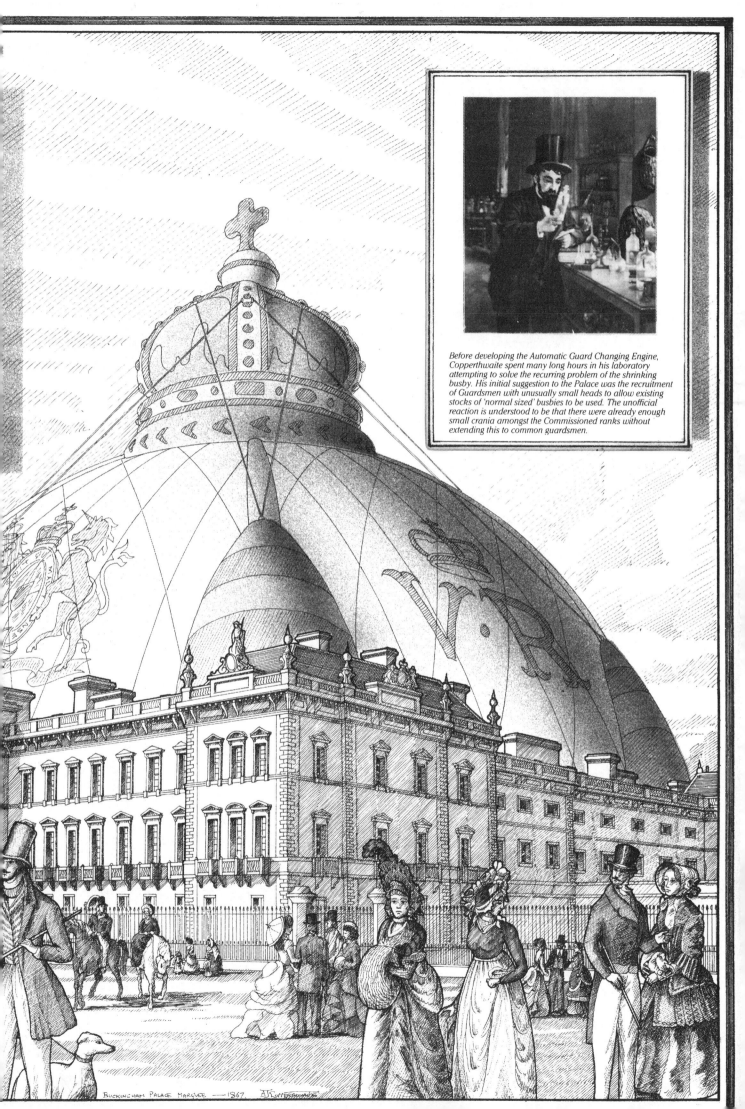

Before developing the Automatic Guard Changing Engine, Copperthwaite spent many long hours in his laboratory attempting to solve the recurring problem of the shrinking busby. His initial suggestion to the Palace was the recruitment of Guardsmen with unusually small heads to allow existing stocks of 'normal sized' busbies to be used. The unofficial reaction is understood to be that there were already enough small crania amongst the Commissioned ranks without extending this to common guardsmen.

BUCKINGHAM PALACE MARQUEE — 1867

CAERNARVON CASTLE CARP FARM & AQUARIUM 1875-1877

Whilst working on his revolutionary new Dirigiplane at Brighton, Copperthwaite took frequent recuperative respites in Wales. It was on one of those 'journeys of mental replenishment' that his diary records his thoughts on the possible use or improvement of Caernarvon Castle.

It was quite obvious to Copperthwaite that the Castle would never serve a useful military purpose again as a fortress due to the devastating powers of the new weapons. He therefore proposed putting the sound and well-built structure to a peaceful and practical use. He would strengthen and seal the walls to make the inner courtyards waterproof. Then he proposed pumping fresh water from nearby streams into the centre of the structure to form a series of artificial lakes. In these lakes he would grow and farm the carp, a much under-rated fish, in his opinion.

It is, he noted in his diaries, an unusually easy fish to breed, and highly nutritious. Eventually, he hoped, his Caernarvon Carp might challenge the Strathspey Salmon in the great seafood restaurants of the world. Though his full plans never materialised, he did arrange for a single courtyard to be sealed and flooded and a modest quantity of fish was produced, although never on a commercial scale. His small scale experiment allowed him to develop his unique Underwater Feeding Suit and the material to write a fascinating recipe book using the carp as the basic ingredient. During the years 1876 to 1880 he wrote one of his many important natural history works, THE CARP: ITS PLAICE IN HISTORY.

After the closure of the Welsh Carp Farm due to a serious leak, Copperthwaite utilized the remaining pools of water to attempt to rear the rare Furry Trout, whose frozen eggs he had brought back from an expedition to Greenland. This piscatorial endeavour was doomed to failure as a Furry Pike egg had inadvertently also been introduced at the same time and the larger hatchling rapidly disposed of all the young naked and defenceless trout.

A cabinet portrait taken of Copperthwaite in the Long Gallery of Caernarvon Castle — the note on the reverse recorded that these fish were the original breeding pair before their introduction to the filter beds.

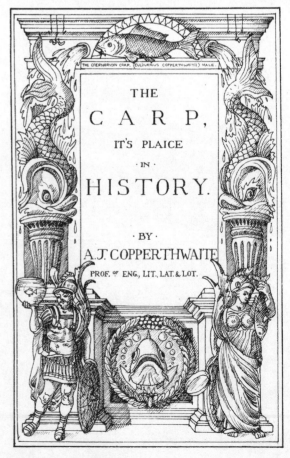

The title page from Copperthwaite's scholarly work on the carp. The title is either one of the worst puns in natural history or yet another example of the Professor's idiosyncratic spelling.

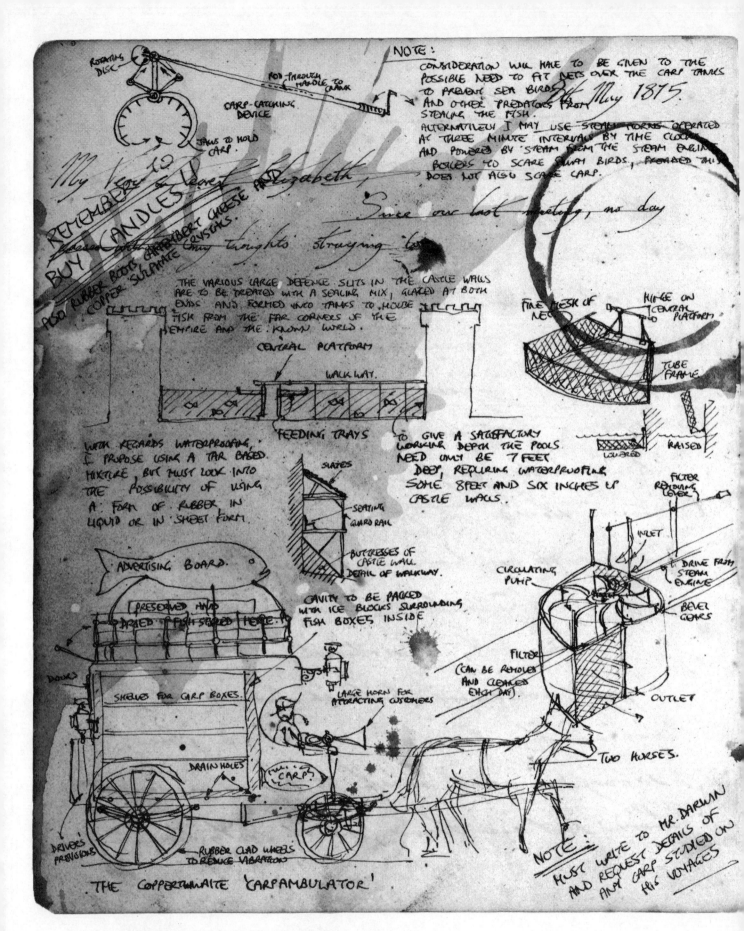

A page from Copperthwaite's Welsh Diaries dated 1875.
Even at this stage he was thinking about actually
marketing the final product with a specially designed
'Carpambulator' delivery waggon.

Opposite — A further page from a later Welsh Diary, this
page dated 1877. A model of a similar diving suit is on
display in the S.A.V.E. exhibition at Fort Regent in Jersey.

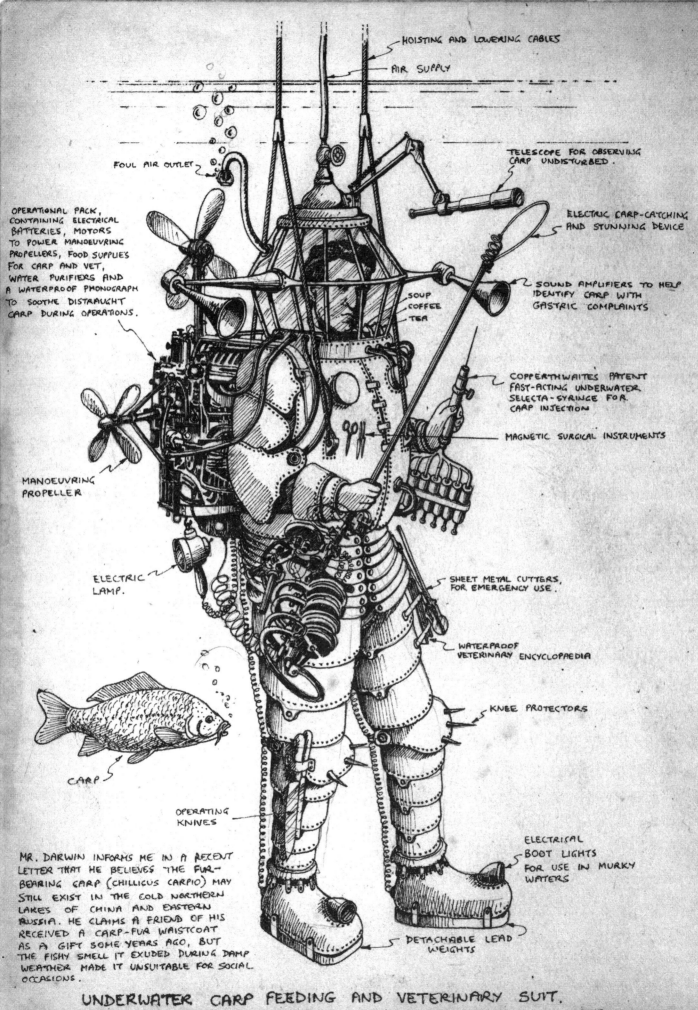

HOISTING AND LOWERING CABLES

AIR SUPPLY

FOUL AIR OUTLET

TELESCOPE FOR OBSERVING CARP UNDISTURBED.

OPERATIONAL PACK, CONTAINING ELECTRICAL BATTERIES, MOTORS TO POWER MANOEUVRING PROPELLERS, FOOD SUPPLIES FOR CARP AND VET, WATER PURIFIERS AND A WATERPROOF PHONOGRAPH TO SOOTHE DISTRAUGHT CARP DURING OPERATIONS.

ELECTRIC CARP-CATCHING AND STUNNING DEVICE

SOUND AMPLIFIERS TO HELP IDENTIFY CARP WITH GASTRIC COMPLAINTS

SOUP
COFFEE
TEA

COPPERTHWAITES PATENT FAST-ACTING UNDERWATER SELECTA-SYRINGE FOR CARP INJECTION

MAGNETIC SURGICAL INSTRUMENTS

MANOEUVRING PROPELLER

ELECTRIC LAMP.

SHEET METAL CUTTERS, FOR EMERGENCY USE.

WATERPROOF VETERINARY ENCYCLOPAEDIA

KNEE PROTECTORS

CARP

OPERATING KNIVES

ELECTRICAL BOOT LIGHTS FOR USE IN MURKY WATERS

MR. DARWIN INFORMS ME IN A RECENT LETTER THAT HE BELIEVES THE FUR-BEARING CARP (CHILLICUS CARPIO) MAY STILL EXIST IN THE COLD NORTHERN LAKES OF CHINA AND EASTERN RUSSIA. HE CLAIMS A FRIEND OF HIS RECEIVED A CARP-FUR WAISTCOAT AS A GIFT SOME YEARS AGO, BUT THE FISHY SMELL IT EXUDED DURING DAMP WEATHER MADE IT UNSUITABLE FOR SOCIAL OCCASIONS.

DETACHABLE LEAD WEIGHTS

UNDERWATER CARP FEEDING AND VETERINARY SUIT.
1877.

AJ Copperthwaite.

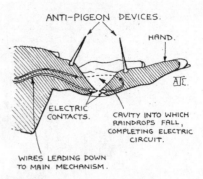

ANTI-PIGEON DEVICES.

HAND.

ELECTRIC
CONTACTS.

CAVITY INTO WHICH
RAINDROPS FALL,
COMPLETING ELECTRIC
CIRCUIT.

WIRES LEADING DOWN
TO MAIN MECHANISM.

SECTION THROUGH
NELSON'S HAND.

*A rare cabinet portrait of Professor Copperthwaite
demonstrating his Nelson's Columbrella prior to a
presentation to the Royal Society of Architects. His mascot
– an Australian Blue-Tongued Skink – is, as always,
looking on.*

NELSON'S COLUMBRELLA
1870-1873

The British climate helped to inspire many of Copperthwaite's designs, but none quite so strongly as his Nelson's Columbrella.

While crossing Trafalgar Square in a heavy rainstorm, he couldn't help noticing how similar in design the column was to a closed umbrella. A plan sprang into his fertile mind, and he rushed back to his rooms to begin work on the huge umbrella plan. Copperthwaite's diaries record that the whole concept and working design took only 'one damp Spring day' to complete and he soon set about raising the funds for the venture. Companies House records reveal the formation of The Columbrella Consortium in 1869 with Professor A J Copperthwaite and Lord Derby amongst the (15) founding shareholders.

The final construction plans specified that in fine weather the umbrella would lie folded against the tower; but as soon as a few drops of rain triggered an electronic circuit in the hand of the statue of Nelson, the umbrella would open and rise majestically to provide 'shelter for more than a hundred souls'.

Construction started as soon as the subscription list was complete and took only some one hundred and forty days to complete. This construction period was not without difficulty and soon Copperthwaite and the sculptor Sir Edward Henry Landseer were at loggerheads over the treatment of the column's base.

Landseer was renowned as the notable stag-at-bay expert and currently enjoyed the position of creator of the lions guarding the base of the column. The story is told of how Copperthwaite, in a furious temper after being insulted 'once too often' by Landseer, broke into his studio whilst the sculptor was 'at bay' somewhere. Copperthwaite found a dejected-looking old lion being used as a model and, taking pity on the creature, poured the entire contents of his hip flask of Old H'ernia into the lion's food bowl. On his return, Landseer couldn't entice the lion to stand up, let alone appear rampant, so he had to model him lying down, as he appears to this day.

ANTI-PIGEON DEVICES.

ELECTRICAL WIRES INSIDE STATUE.

PROPOSED NEW STATUE OF NELSON.

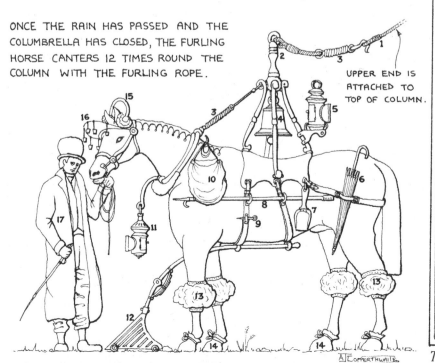

ONCE THE RAIN HAS PASSED AND THE COLUMBRELLA HAS CLOSED, THE FURLING HORSE CANTERS 12 TIMES ROUND THE COLUMN WITH THE FURLING ROPE.

UPPER END IS ATTACHED TO TOP OF COLUMN.

1. FURLING ROPE.
2. SWIVEL.
3. COIL SPRINGS.
4. BELL TO WARN PEDESTRIANS OF APPROACHING HORSE.
5. REAR LAMP.
6. UMBRELLA FOR ATTENDANT.
7. SHOVEL (MISC.)
8. FURLING ROPE DISCONNECTOR.
9. THING FOR GETTING STONES OUT OF HOOVES.
10. FOOD BAG OF OATS.
11. HEAD LAMP.
12. 'DOVECATCHER' TO SAFELY REMOVE PIGEONS FROM PATH OF GALLOPING HORSE.
13. PADDING TO AVOID INJURIES ON TIGHT CORNERS.
14. NON-SLIP WATERPROOF SHOES.
15. ANTI-PANNIC EAR MUFFS FOR THUNDER STORMS.
16. RAIN SHIELD WITH ANTI-HORSE-FLY CORKS.
17. HORSE ATTENDANT.

The furling horse.

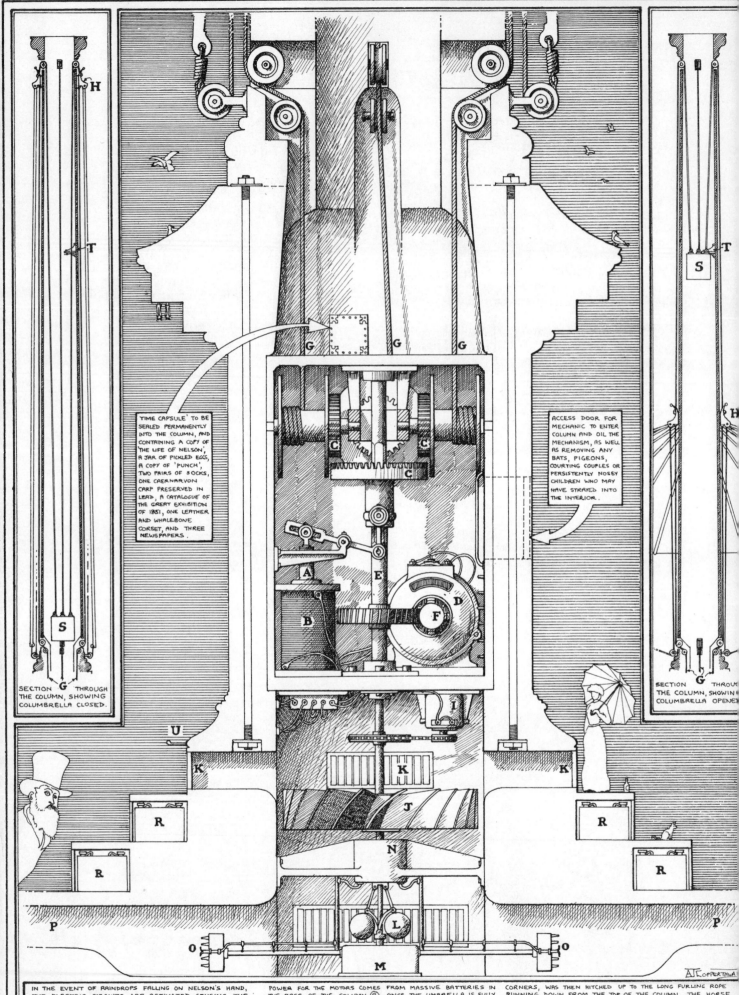

TIME CAPSULE TO BE SEALED PERMANENTLY INTO THE COLUMN, AND CONTAINING A COPY OF 'THE LIFE OF NELSON', A JAR OF PICKLED EGGS, A COPY OF 'PUNCH', TWO PAIRS OF SOCKS, ONE CAERNARVON CARP PRESERVED IN LEAD, A CATALOGUE OF THE GREAT EXHIBITION OF 1851, ONE LEATHER AND WHALEBONE CORSET, AND THREE NEWSPAPERS.

ACCESS DOOR FOR MECHANIC TO ENTER COLUMN AND OIL THE MECHANISM, AS WELL AS REMOVING ANY BATS, PIGEONS, COURTING COUPLES OR PERSISTENTLY NOSEY CHILDREN WHO MAY HAVE STRAYED INTO THE INTERIOR.

SECTION THROUGH THE COLUMN, SHOWING COLUMBRELLA CLOSED.

SECTION THROUGH THE COLUMN, SHOWING COLUMBRELLA OPENED.

IN THE EVENT OF RAINDROPS FALLING ON NELSON'S HAND, THE ELECTRIC CIRCUITS ARE ACTIVATED, CAUSING THE PLUNGER (A) TO BE DRAWN IN BY THE ELECTRIC COIL (B) THUS ENGAGING THE GEARS (C). AT THE SAME MOMENT THE MAIN ELECTRIC MOTOR (D) STARTS, AND TURNS THE SHAFT (E) THROUGH A WORM GEAR (F) THUS WINDING IN THE CABLES (G). THESE DRAW THE TOP FRAME OF THE UMBRELLA (H) DOWN AND CAUSE IT TO OPEN. THE SMALLER ELECTRIC MOTOR (I) DRIVES A FAN (J) WHICH SUCKS IN AIR AT (K). AT THE SAME TIME A GOVERNOR ON THE FAN SHAFT (L) OPENS THE GAS SUPPLY (M) AND A GENERATOR (N) PROVIDES POWER FOR A SPARK AT (O) TO IGNITE THE GAS FLAMES. THUS WARM AIR IS FORCED OUT BY THE FAN AT (P) TO DRY THE SHELTERING POPULACE.

POWER FOR THE MOTORS COMES FROM MASSIVE BATTERIES IN THE BASE OF THE COLUMN, (R). ONCE THE UMBRELLA IS FULLY OPENED, THE RISING COUNTERBALANCE WEIGHTS (S) COME INTO CONTACT WITH A CUT-OFF SWITCH (T) WHICH IMMEDIATELY STOPS THE MAIN ELECTRIC MOTOR. THE COIL (B) ENGAGING THE GEARS, AND THE FAN (J) CONTINUE TO WORK HOWEVER. THEY ONLY SHUT OFF WHEN THE RAIN HAS STOPPED AND THE CONTACTS IN NELSON'S HAND ARE FREE OF MOISTURE. AT THAT TIME THE PLUNGER (A) IS RELEASED BY THE COIL (B) AND THE CABLES (G) ARE FREE TO UNWIND. INSIDE THE COLUMN THE COUNTER-BALANCE WEIGHTS, HEAVIER THAN THE UMBRELLA, DRAW IT BACK UP INTO THE CLOSED POSITION. THE FURLING HORSE, A THOROUGHBRED NOTED FOR ITS ABILITY TO TURN SHARP

CORNERS, WAS THEN HITCHED UP TO THE LONG FURLING ROPE RUNNING DOWN FROM THE TOP OF THE COLUMN. THE HORSE GALLOPED TWELVE TIMES ROUND THE COLUMN TO WRAP THE FURLING ROPE TIGHTLY AND PREVENT WIND DAMAGE TO THE UMBRELLA. THE END OF THE FURLING ROPE WAS HITCHED ONTO THE PIN (U) FROM WHICH IT COULD EASILY BE REMOVED BY THE MECHANICAL OPENING OF THE UMBRELLA. THE UNDER SURFACE OF THE UMBRELLA IS DECORATED WITH SCENES DEPICTING FAMOUS BRITISH VICTORIES AND DEEDS, ENABLING THE POPULACE TO ADMIRE THE QUALITIES OF THE GREAT MEN AND WOMEN OF THE PAST, WHILE SHELTERING FROM THE ELEMENTS.

A.T. COPPERTHWAITE

NELSON'S COLUMBRELLA: LONDON: 1873.

COPPERTHWAITES PERSONALISED COLUMBRELLA

COPPERTHWAITES GARDEN COLUMBRELLA

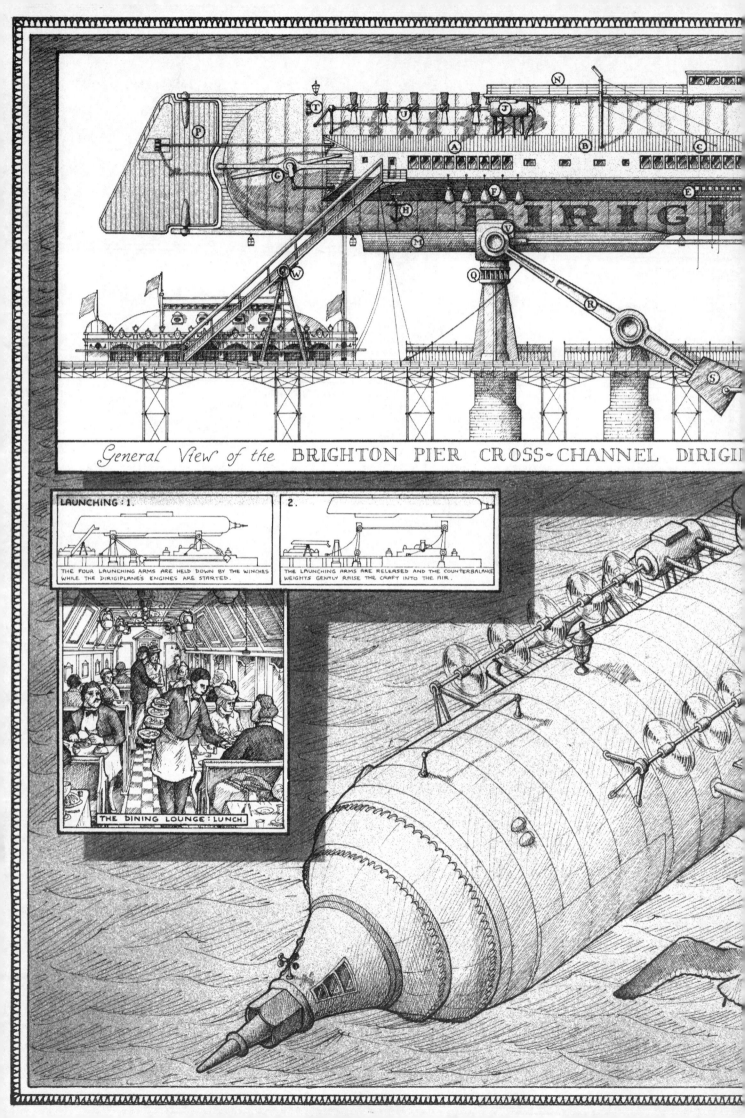

General View of the BRIGHTON PIER CROSS~CHANNEL DIRIGI

LAUNCHING : 1.

THE FOUR LAUNCHING ARMS ARE HELD DOWN BY THE WINCHES WHILE THE DIRIGIPLANE'S ENGINES ARE STARTED.

2.

THE LAUNCHING ARMS ARE RELEASED AND THE COUNTERBALANCE WEIGHTS GENTLY RAISE THE CRAFT INTO THE AIR.

THE DINING LOUNGE : LUNCH.

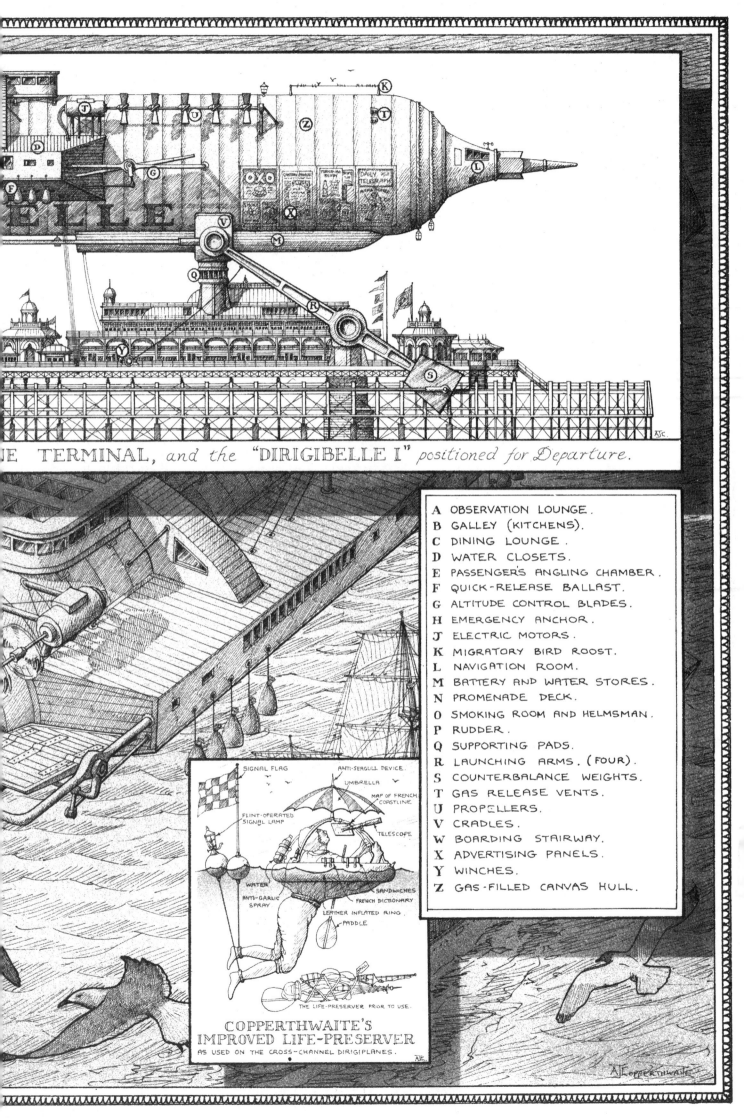

JE TERMINAL, *and the* "DIRIGIBELLE I" *positioned for Departure.*

A OBSERVATION LOUNGE.
B GALLEY (KITCHENS).
C DINING LOUNGE.
D WATER CLOSETS.
E PASSENGER'S ANGLING CHAMBER.
F QUICK-RELEASE BALLAST.
G ALTITUDE CONTROL BLADES.
H EMERGENCY ANCHOR.
J ELECTRIC MOTORS.
K MIGRATORY BIRD ROOST.
L NAVIGATION ROOM.
M BATTERY AND WATER STORES.
N PROMENADE DECK.
O SMOKING ROOM AND HELMSMAN.
P RUDDER.
Q SUPPORTING PADS.
R LAUNCHING ARMS. (FOUR).
S COUNTERBALANCE WEIGHTS.
T GAS RELEASE VENTS.
U PROPELLERS.
V CRADLES.
W BOARDING STAIRWAY.
X ADVERTISING PANELS.
Y WINCHES.
Z GAS-FILLED CANVAS HULL.

SIGNAL FLAG
ANTI-SEAGULL DEVICE.
UMBRELLA
MAP OF FRENCH COASTLINE.
FLINT-OPERATED SIGNAL LAMP
TELESCOPE
WATER
SANDWICHES
ANTI-GARLIC SPRAY
FRENCH DICTIONARY
LEATHER INFLATED RING
PADDLE
THE LIFE-PRESERVER PRIOR TO USE.

COPPERTHWAITE'S
IMPROVED LIFE-PRESERVER
AS USED ON THE CROSS-CHANNEL DIRIGIPLANES.

BRIGHTON PIER CROSS-CHANNEL DIRIGIPLANE TERMINAL 1876-1879

In the 1870's and 1880's many individuals of pioneering spirit were experimenting with flight. Some favoured the glider or heavier-than-air-machine, while others favoured the balloon. Professor Copperthwaite decided to combine the best qualities of each in his unique 'Dirigiplanes'.

He planned a regular service across the English Channel, with four Dirigiplane operating at the same time. To reduce the length of the flight and the risks of flying over land, he planned to strengthen and use Brighton Pier, making a take-off strip above the actual walkway of the pier. A catapult system would fire the craft with its forty passengers out over the waters of the Channel, while a steam crane lifted the returning Dirigiplane out of the water and back onto the launch track again. The idea caused much excitement among early flying enthusiasts, but the scheme was initially delayed due to the difficulty of finding a suitable pier in France for the return launchings.

Today there are those who claim that Copperthwaite's Dirigiplanes were possibly the inspiration for the hovercraft that now travel regularly across the Channel. In fact, many of the facilities devised by Copperthwaite in the construction of the *Dirigibelle I* and her sister craft are still found in modern cross-channel transport − the advertising panels, suggested by his life-long friend Hamish McSaatchi; the appalling food on the journey and disgusting state of the water closets, the latter caused, the Dirigiplane Company insisted, by the rapid upwards motion of the launching arms at take-off.

The Professor was especially conscious of safety at sea in the unlikely (he insisted) event of a ditching in the Channel − or even channelling in a ditch. His 'Improved Life Preserver' incorporated many innovative features which could be profitably used today. His drawings of this clever device illustrate the quality of invention of which Britain can still be justly proud. In its original form, the thirty page book of *'Instructions for Use in an Emergency'* possibly limited its practical effectiveness. In the first official trial of the Life Preserver for the Sea Lords, the leather-bound 'Instructions' became rapidly saturated and its weight dragged the 'victim' to the bottom of the Serpentine.

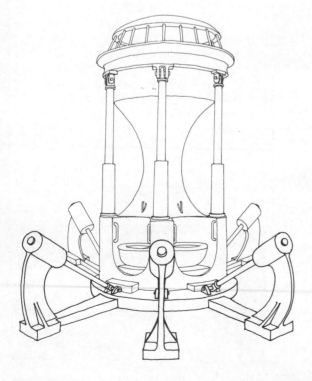

The unique gyroscopic Copperthwaite Four-Seater Water Closet. This was complete with hydrostatic compensating rams which allowed it (in theory at least! Ed) to be used during launching of the 'Dirigibelle 1'. The water storage tank in the head of the closet was also hinged to prevent spillage over occupants.

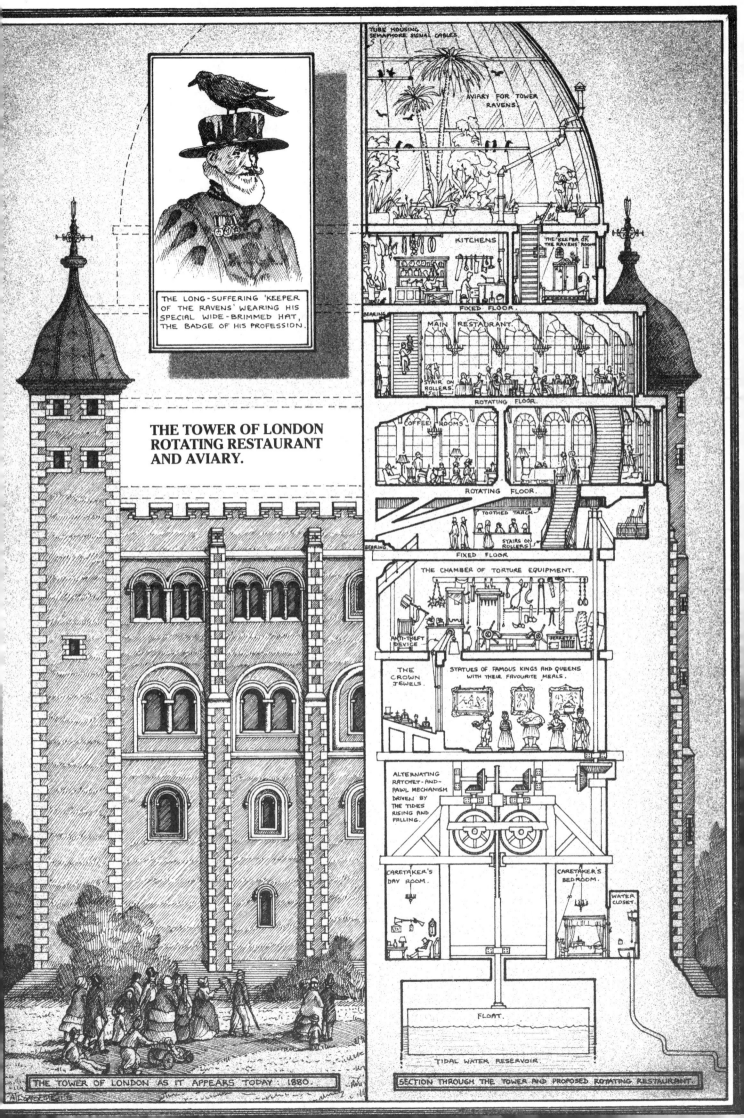

THE LONG-SUFFERING 'KEEPER OF THE RAVENS' WEARING HIS SPECIAL WIDE-BRIMMED HAT, THE BADGE OF HIS PROFESSION.

THE TOWER OF LONDON ROTATING RESTAURANT AND AVIARY.

TUBE HOUSING SEMAPHORE SIGNAL CABLES.

AVIARY FOR TOWER RAVENS.

KITCHENS

THE 'KEEPER OF THE RAVENS' ROOM.

FIXED FLOOR.

BEARING.

MAIN RESTAURANT.

STAIR ON ROLLERS.

ROTATING FLOOR.

COFFEE ROOMS

ROTATING FLOOR.

TOOTHED TRACK

STAIRS ON ROLLERS.

BEARING.

FIXED FLOOR.

THE CHAMBER OF TORTURE EQUIPMENT.

ANTI-THEFT DEVICE

THE CROWN JEWELS.

STATUES OF FAMOUS KINGS AND QUEENS WITH THEIR FAVOURITE MEALS.

ALTERNATING RATCHET-AND-PAWL MECHANISM DRIVEN BY THE TIDES RISING AND FALLING.

CARETAKER'S DAY ROOM.

CARETAKER'S BEDROOM.

WATER CLOSET.

FLOAT.

TIDAL WATER RESERVOIR.

THE TOWER OF LONDON AS IT APPEARS TODAY: 1880.

SECTION THROUGH THE TOWER AND PROPOSED ROTATING RESTAURANT.

APPLICANTS FOR THE JOB OF 'RESTAURANT ENTERTAINERS'

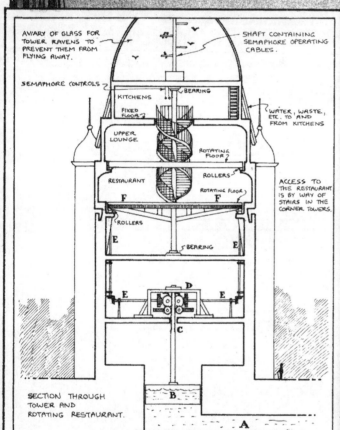

AVIARY OF GLASS FOR TOWER RAVENS TO PREVENT THEM FROM FLYING AWAY.

SHAFT CONTAINING SEMAPHORE OPERATING CABLES.

SEMAPHORE CONTROLS

BEARING

KITCHENS

FIXED FLOOR

WATER, WASTE, ETC. TO AND FROM KITCHENS

UPPER LOUNGE

ROTATING FLOOR

RESTAURANT

ROLLERS

ROTATING FLOOR

F

F

ACCESS TO THE RESTAURANT IS BY WAY OF STAIRS IN THE CORNER TOWERS.

ROLLERS

E

E

BEARING

E

D

E

E

C

SECTION THROUGH TOWER AND ROTATING RESTAURANT.

B

A

THE RISING AND FALLING OF THE TIDE ON THE THAMES CAUSES WATER TO FLOW UP AND DOWN THE CHANNEL (A) AND RAISES AND LOWERS THE MASSIVE FLOAT (B). BY WAY OF THE TOOTHED RACK (C) THIS ACTIVATES THE GEARS (D) WHICH IN TURN ROTATE THE CONNECTING RODS (E). AT THE UPPER END OF THESE RODS ARE GEARS WHICH MESH WITH THE TEETH ROUND THE RIM OF THE REVOLVING RESTAURANT FLOOR (F) TURNING IT ONCE EVERY 6 HOURS.

ROTATING RESTAURANT SPECIALITIES

'CROMWELL'S HEAD' (WILD BOAR IN ARMOUR)

'RAREBIT-ON-THE-RACK' (HOT CHEESE STRETCHED PAINFULLY BETWEEN TWO SAUSAGES OVER TOAST)

'THE SIX WIVES OF HENRY VIII' (A SELECTION OF WARM AFTER-DINNER TARTS.)

'JUGGED HEIR' (IN MEMORY OF MARY, QUEEN OF SCOTS.)

TRAINING WAITERS TO COPE WITH THE LUNCHTIME RUSH. 1881.

SKETCH OF THE RESTAURANT INTERIOR. 1881.

BY A FRIEND OF TOULOUSE LAUTREC'S LANDLADY.

SPECIAL SIGNALS (2)

'NO DOGS'

SPECIAL SIGNALS (4)

'ONLY IN SEASON'

THE TOWER OF LONDON ROTATING RESTAURANT AND AVIARY: 1881.

WITH SEMAPHORE SIGNALLING DEVICE TO GIVE DETAILS OF THE DAY'S MENU TO THE POPULACE. A.T. Copperthwaite

TOWER OF LONDON
ROTATING RESTAURANT & AVIARY
1880-1881

Copperthwaite was a life-long gourmet and lover of the good life. When enjoying supper in the Trocadero, a fellow guest begged him to turn his 'multi-faceted talents' to create 'an eating place worthy of our great city'.

At this time the White Tower (better known as the Tower of London) was sadly neglected and scheduled for renovation. Copperthwaite proposed building a rotating restaurant on top of the White Tower. It would also incorporate a glass-walled aviary to house the Tower's ravens and encourage them to breed.

The restaurant would be rotated slowly by the rising and falling tides of the nearby River Thames using a system of massive floats, huge gears and connecting rods.

On the very top of the structure, visible for miles around, Copperthwaite planned to construct a large semaphore system. This would continuously transmit the day's menu, enabling visitors to decide what they would have to eat whilst on the journey to the restaurant. Free semaphore guides were issued thoughout London a week before the restaurant opened in 1881. Specially trained carrier pigeons flew copies of the first day's specialities to the leading lights of London society. Rather ungratefully, these menus included an invitation to bring 'the bearer back poste-haste to the Tower to be prepared in an entertaining variety of exotic sauces'.

The Rotating Restaurant quickly caught the imagination of London society being patronised by captains of industry, poets, writers and artists. Not surprisingly it was chosen as the luncheon rooms for the newly formed Rotary Club. The young Oscar Wilde, recently down from Oxford, became a frequent observer of the auditions for waiters selecting the 'fleet of foot and limp of wrist' and those of 'unusual physique'. It was evidently an advantage to have one leg shorter than the other as this assisted in carrying spit-roasted Rota-Burgers in a continually circulating room. The 'RR' was also adopted by hostesses as a fashionable venue for private functions and gave rise to the expression 'See you around!'

Frequent problems with the rotating motion occurred when engine room artificers supped too deeply in the neighbouring wine cellars and mistook the main speed control for a similar-looking cork extractor. Many guests confirmed that the increased motion of the Restaurant added an exciting dimension as they entertained actresses in private dining rooms.

Copperthwaite's interest did not wane when his creation opened to wide acclaim. He then spent 'productive hours' in the kitchens experimenting with a variety of unique dishes especially for the Rotating Restaurant. Enthusiasm for the new establishment was not, however, universal and some coffee house wags combined its movement and quality of cuisine, in dubbing it 'The Thames-Side Spit'.

Title page of Copperthwaite's journal 'Around the World with Rod and Glass' – the full record of his natural history travels in the period 1856 to 1878.

FORTH RAILWAY BRIDGE WHISKY STORE & DISTILLERY 1890-1893

Like many travellers at the time, Professor Copperthwaite marvelled at the newly completed Forth Railway Bridge when he travelled in Scotland in the winter of 1890. However he visualised the structure as something more than just a bridge. The gigantic cylindrical pillars of the bridge were hollow, and capable of containing thousands of gallons of liquid . . . but what liquid? Looking up he noticed an advertisement in his carriage; whisky! That was it! So close to the Scottish capital, and yet so secure, the bridge would make an excellent whisky store and distillery.

He planned a distillery on the little island of Inch Garvie, once a fortress, and now the support for the northern-most span of the bridge. From the distillery the whisky would be pumped directly into the bridge. The insides of the huge columns would have to be lined with sherry-soaked veneer to enhance the whisky flavour. Copperthwaite returned to The Bridge in 1891, and set up the first still on the island of Inch Garvie. A prefabricated oak tank was shipped up in the schooner 'Wee Doch and Doris' from Whitby, and the newly distilled whisky pumped in. The resultant amber-pink liquor was an immediate success and achieved almost instant popularity with Scottish tipplers. Its popularity may well have been due to its unique flavour (being filtered through gunpowder) and highly distinctive colour — this latter feature due, in part, to the joint effects of oak-lined tubes coupled with liberal applications of red oxide paint.

Legend has it that some 800 gallons of the unique amber-pink liquid remain to this day sealed-up in the bridge uprights, according to Scottish Customs & Excise confidential records.

This fact may explain why one of the most legendary maintenance jobs in the world — the continual re-painting of the Forth Bridge — is seldom short of willing recruits. Occasionally men can be seen, on the pretext of scraping rust on the Bridge, tapping away with paint chippers, always listening for the dull 'CLUNK' to replace the hollow echo that will indicate the presence of that 800 gallons of liquid gold.

Any seepage of liquid from the Bridge may also explain the distinctive flavour of kippers caught down river (especially on a neap tide) which are offered as an occasional local delicacy at the nearby Cramond Inn Restaurant.

Bottle of Copperthwaite's Old H'ernia whisky found and sampled recently when the Readfern National Glass factory in York was demolished in 1986.

41

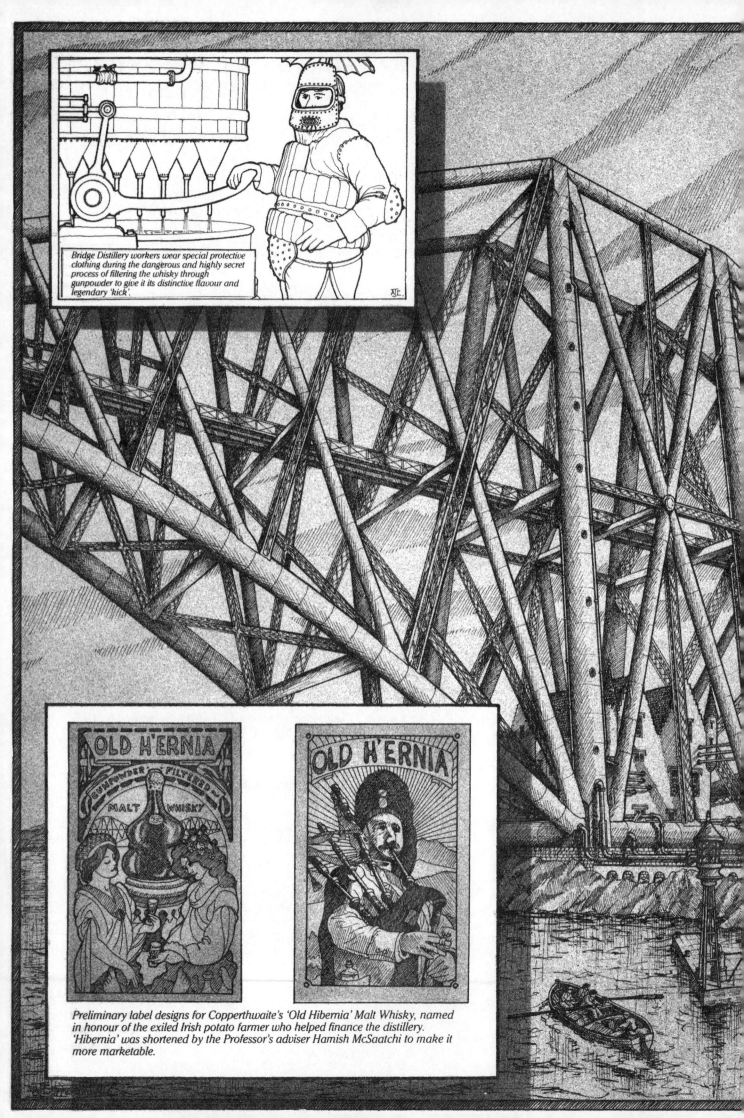

Bridge Distillery workers wear special protective clothing during the dangerous and highly secret process of filtering the whisky through gunpowder to give it its distinctive flavour and legendary 'kick'.

Preliminary label designs for Copperthwaite's 'Old Hibernia' Malt Whisky, named in honour of the exiled Irish potato farmer who helped finance the distillery. 'Hibernia' was shortened by the Professor's adviser Hamish McSaatchi to make it more marketable.

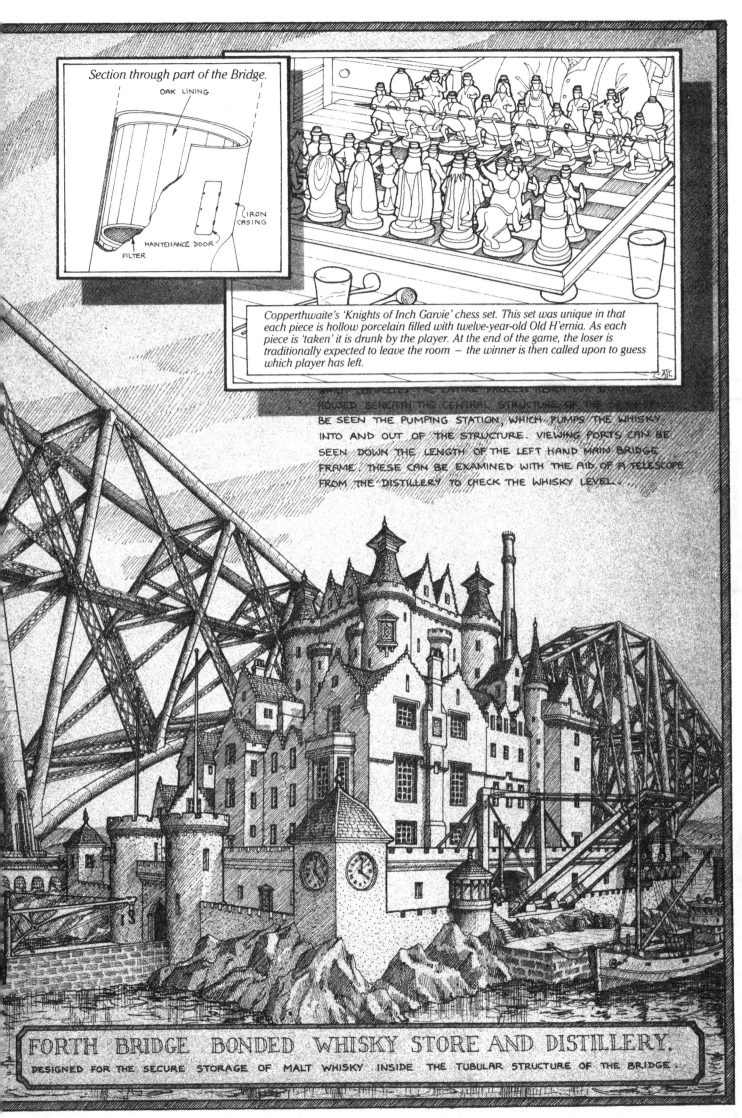

Section through part of the Bridge.

OAK LINING.

IRON CASING

MAINTENANCE DOOR

FILTER

Copperthwaite's 'Knights of Inch Garvie' chess set. This set was unique in that each piece is hollow porcelain filled with twelve-year-old Old H'ernia. As each piece is 'taken' it is drunk by the player. At the end of the game, the loser is traditionally expected to leave the room — the winner is then called upon to guess which player has left.

...HOUSED BENEATH THE CENTRAL STRUCTURE OF THE... BE SEEN THE PUMPING STATION, WHICH PUMPS THE WHISKY INTO AND OUT OF THE STRUCTURE. VIEWING PORTS CAN BE SEEN DOWN THE LENGTH OF THE LEFT HAND MAIN BRIDGE FRAME. THESE CAN BE EXAMINED WITH THE AID OF A TELESCOPE FROM THE DISTILLERY TO CHECK THE WHISKY LEVEL.

FORTH BRIDGE BONDED WHISKY STORE AND DISTILLERY.
DESIGNED FOR THE SECURE STORAGE OF MALT WHISKY INSIDE THE TUBULAR STRUCTURE OF THE BRIDGE.

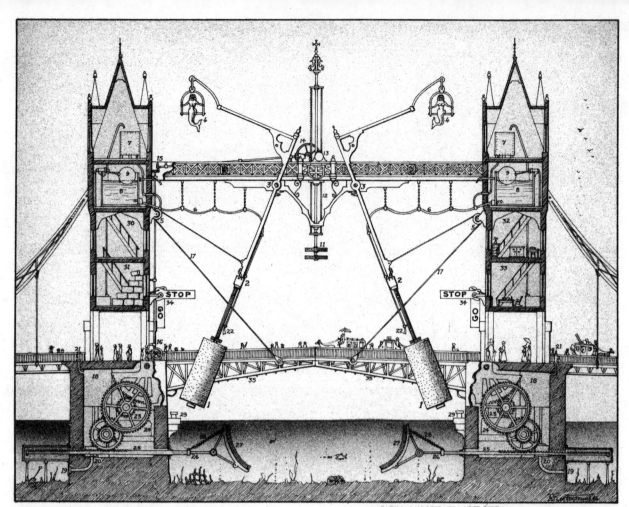

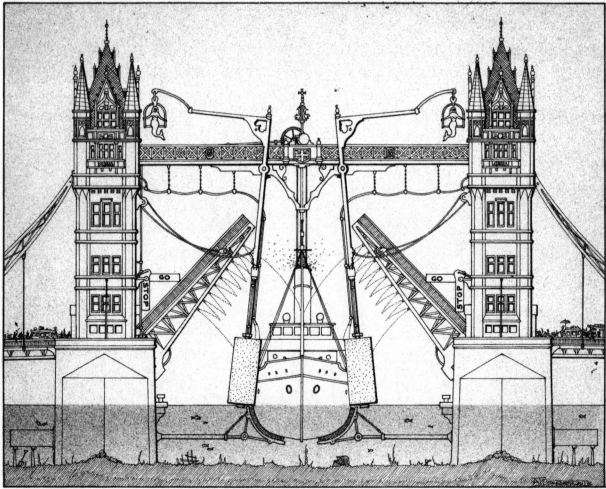

How the Boat-Wash works . . .

A vessel approaching the Boat-Wash is first halted by the ticket collector. There are two ticket collectors, one operating upstream and one downstream. Each has a raft fitted to the end of a long companionway enabling the structure to float well out into mid-stream. The inner ends of the two companionways fit onto pivots (29) at the base of the bridge towers.

As the two sections of the bridge (35) open, the cables (17) become slack, allowing the cleaning brushes (1) to fall against the sides of the entering ship. The counter-balance mermaids (4) hold the brushes tightly against the ship's sides. The electric switches (3) are triggered, starting the motors (2) which drive the bushes (1); at the same time the rising of the bridge sections (35) operates a series of gears (23) which wind the underwater scouring brushes (27) into position by means of a toothed rack (25). The switches (3) also trigger electric valves to release water (8) and liquid soap (7) into the pipes (6) leading to nozzles (22) above the rotating brushes. Separate pumps (20) draw in water through filters (19) and supply a powerful spray to the nozzles on the undersides of the bridge sections (35) giving the ship's decks a good wash. The interior of the funnels can be scoured clean by wire brushes (11) lowered by means of gearing (14) & (15) and a hand winch (16) while an electric motor turns the brushes at great speed (13).

Other features include:

(30) Temporary accommodation for ship's stowaways.	*(32) Office and safe room for cash.*	*(24) Main hydraulic motors to open bridge.*
(31) Chamois leather cloth store, for sale to dry their portholes.	*(33) Bridge Master's day room and rest room.*	*(9) The world's largest ball-valves.*
	(18) Main liquid soap vats.	

TOWER BRIDGE SAIL-THROUGH BOATWASH 1896-1897

Returning in 1896, from one of his trips to the far-flung corners of the British Empire, Copperthwaite could not help but notice the grimy, sea-worn state of his little vessel after her long journey. As he looked around this Port of London he saw that most of the examples of our proud maritime fleet were in the same sad condition.

As he sailed under the new Tower Bridge, his mind visualised the span of the bridge as two welcoming arms. 'How easily', he thought to himself, 'could those arms be adapted to clean the home-coming ships as they passed through!' This simple idea developed into one of the most successful designs – The Tower Bridge Sail-Through Boatwash. He constructed a large working model showing how, as the bridge opened, spinning brushes scoured the hull clean with the help of powerful jets of water. Coarse wire brushes rose from below the surface to scour off the barnacle and growth at the same time. Even re-painting could be carried out as the ship sailed through, without even stopping! All the water, paint, detergent etc. was to be stored in tanks in the two main towers of the bridge.

Copperthwaite demonstrated his superb working model to London's Bridge Masters and they were so impressed, he records, not only by the ingenious use of their latest bridge but also with the potential extra revenue to be raised that the scheme was quickly adopted.

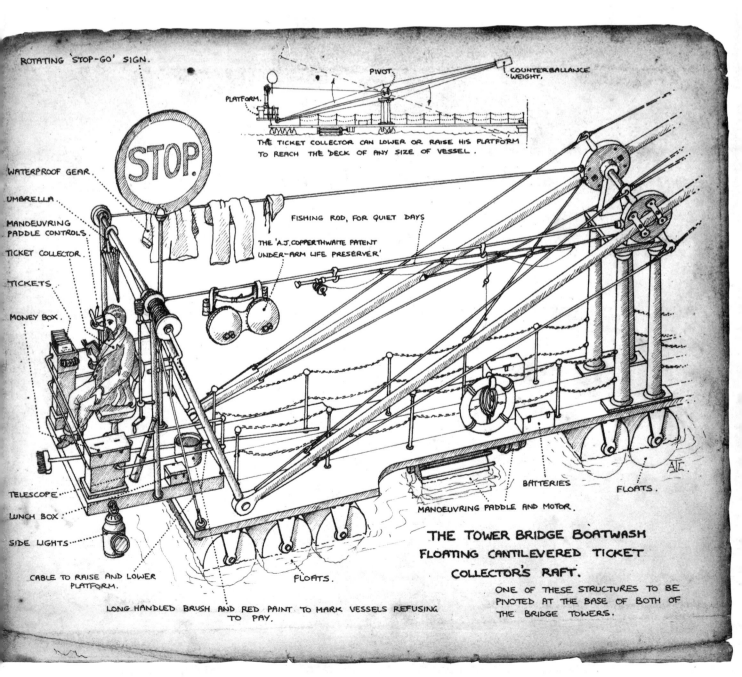

ROTATING 'STOP-GO' SIGN.

PLATFORM.

PIVOT.

COUNTERBALANCE WEIGHT.

THE TICKET COLLECTOR CAN LOWER OR RAISE HIS PLATFORM TO REACH THE DECK OF ANY SIZE OF VESSEL.

WATERPROOF GEAR.

UMBRELLA.

MANOEUVRING PADDLE CONTROLS.

TICKET COLLECTOR.

TICKETS.

MONEY BOX.

FISHING ROD, FOR QUIET DAYS

THE 'A.J. COPPERTHWAITE PATENT UNDER-ARM LIFE PRESERVER'

TELESCOPE.

LUNCH BOX.

SIDE LIGHTS.

CABLE TO RAISE AND LOWER PLATFORM.

FLOATS.

LONG HANDLED BRUSH AND RED PAINT TO MARK VESSELS REFUSING TO PAY.

BATTERIES

FLOATS.

MANOEUVRING PADDLE AND MOTOR.

THE TOWER BRIDGE BOATWASH FLOATING CANTILEVERED TICKET COLLECTOR'S RAFT.

ONE OF THESE STRUCTURES TO BE PIVOTED AT THE BASE OF BOTH OF THE BRIDGE TOWERS.

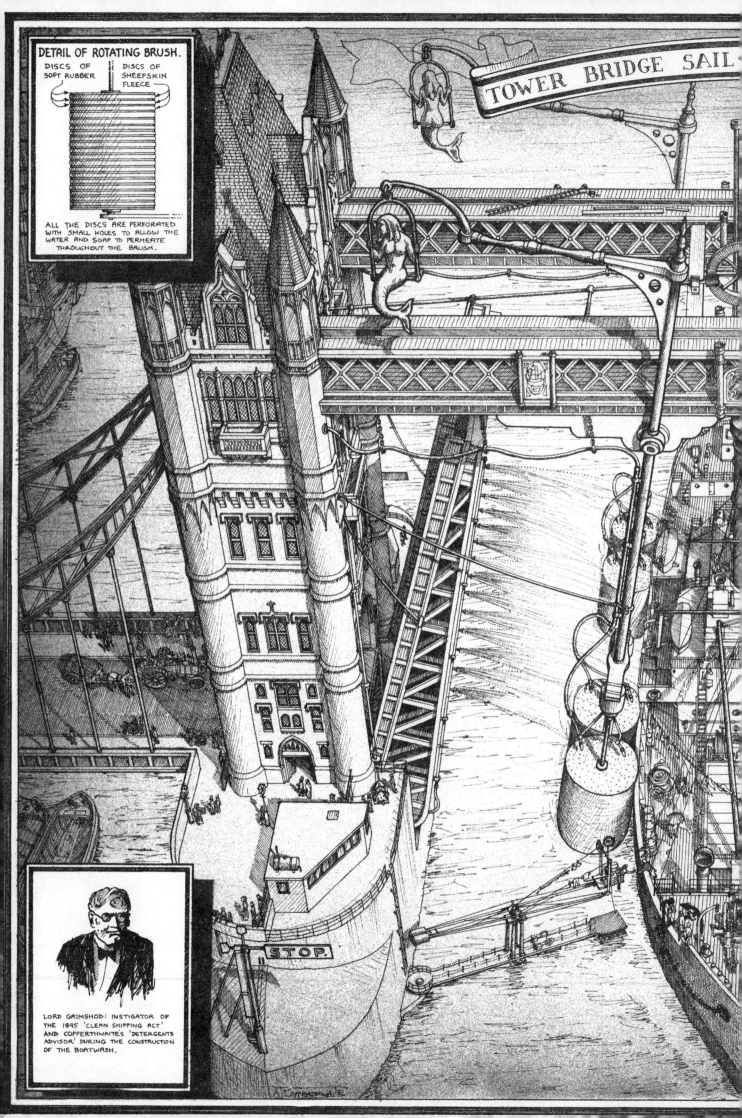

DETAIL OF ROTATING BRUSH.

DISCS OF SOFT RUBBER   DISCS OF SHEEPSKIN FLEECE

ALL THE DISCS ARE PERFORATED WITH SMALL HOLES TO ALLOW THE WATER AND SOAP TO PERMEATE THROUGHOUT THE BRUSH.

TOWER BRIDGE SAIL

STOP.

LORD GRIMSHOD: INSTIGATOR OF THE 1895 'CLEAN SHIPPING ACT' AND COPPERTHWAITE'S 'DETERGENTS ADVISOR' DURING THE CONSTRUCTION OF THE BOATWASH.

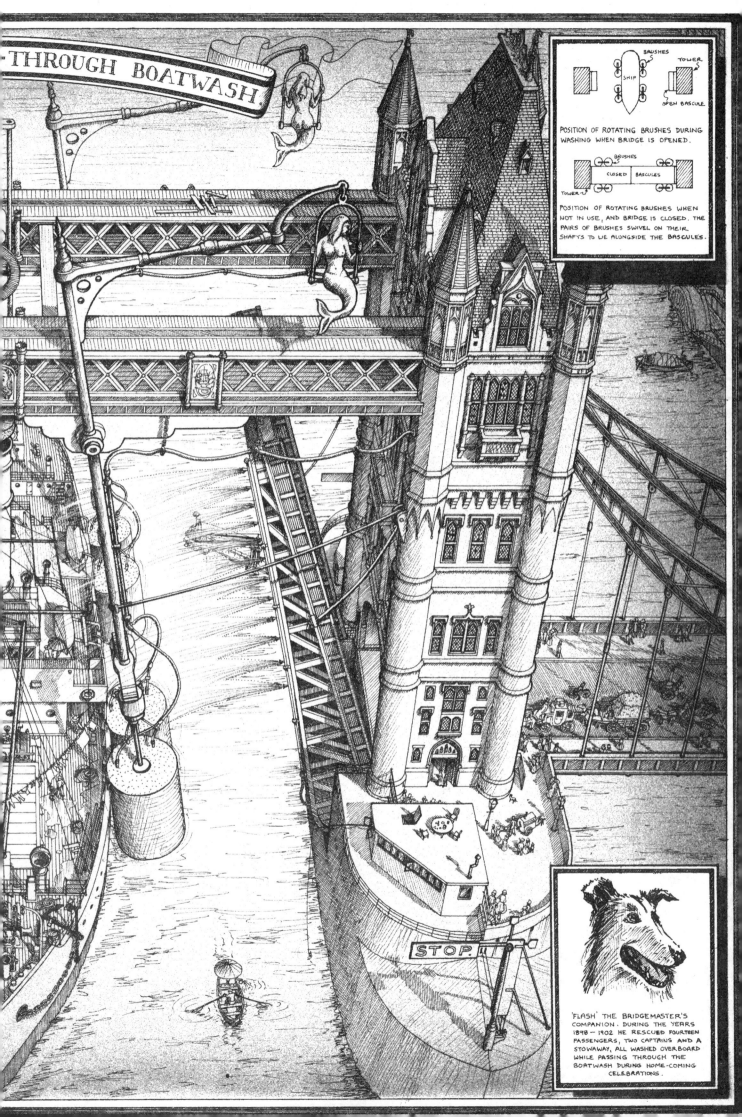

THROUGH BOATWASH.

POSITION OF ROTATING BRUSHES DURING WASHING WHEN BRIDGE IS OPENED.

POSITION OF ROTATING BRUSHES WHEN NOT IN USE, AND BRIDGE IS CLOSED. THE PAIRS OF BRUSHES SWIVEL ON THEIR SHAFTS TO LIE ALONGSIDE THE BASCULES.

STOP.

'FLASH' THE BRIDGEMASTER'S COMPANION. DURING THE YEARS 1898 – 1902 HE RESCUED FOURTEEN PASSENGERS, TWO CAPTAINS AND A STOWAWAY, ALL WASHED OVERBOARD WHILE PASSING THROUGH THE BOATWASH DURING HOME-COMING CELEBRATIONS.

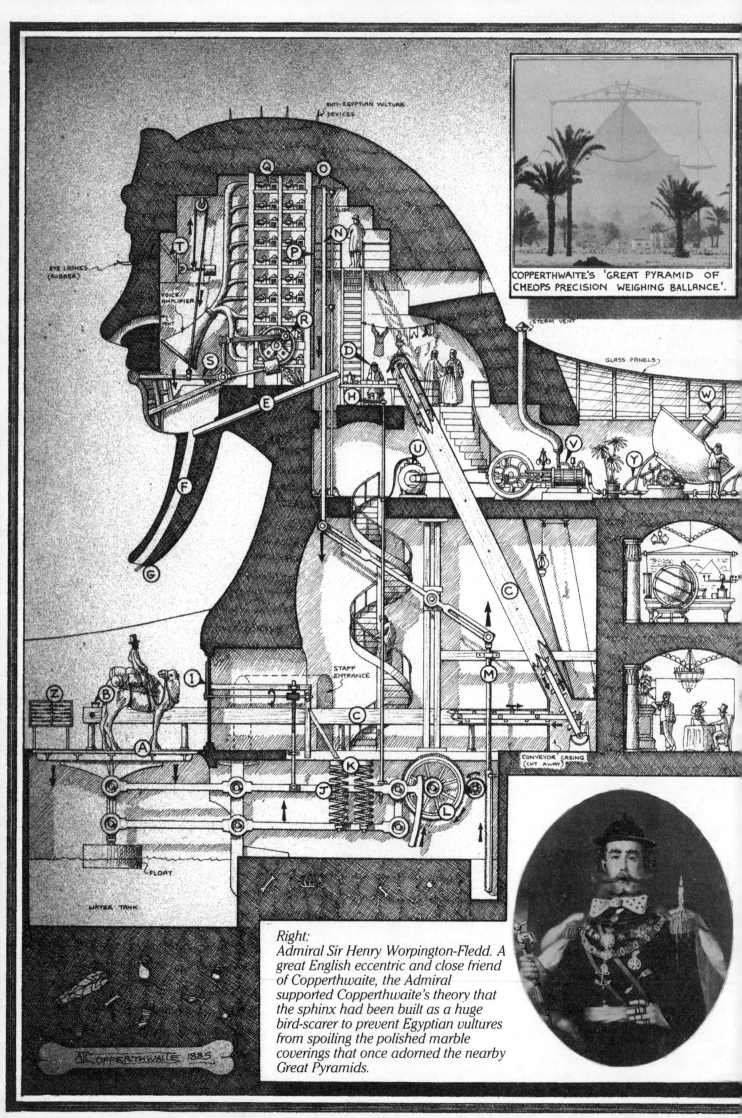

ANTI-EGYPTIAN VULTURE DEVICES

EYE LASHES (RUBBER)

VOICE AMPLIFIER

COPPERTHWAITE'S 'GREAT PYRAMID OF CHEOPS PRECISION WEIGHING BALLANCE'.

STEAM VENT

GLASS PANELS

STAFF ENTRANCE

CONVEYOR CASING (CUT AWAY)

WATER TANK

FLOAT

A.T. COPPERTHWAITE 1885

Right:
Admiral Sir Henry Worpington-Fledd. A great English eccentric and close friend of Copperthwaite, the Admiral supported Copperthwaite's theory that the sphinx had been built as a huge bird-scarer to prevent Egyptian vultures from spoiling the polished marble coverings that once adorned the nearby Great Pyramids.

THE SPHINX AS SHE APPEARS TODAY.

I SPEAK YOUR WEIGHT

THE SPHINX AFTER COPPERTHWAITE'S CONVERSION.

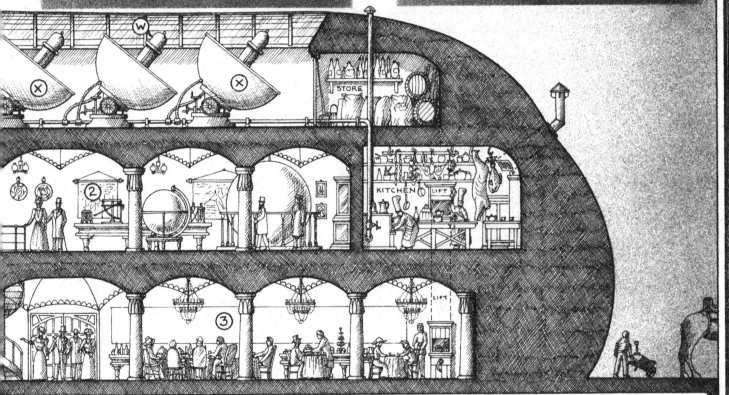

THE SPHINX SOLAR POWERED 'I SPEAK YOUR WEIGHT' MACHINE.

THOSE WISHING TO BE WEIGHED FIRST STEP ONTO THE WEIGHING PLATFORM (A) AND PLACE THEIR MONEY IN THE PAYMENT BOX (B). FROM HERE THE CONVEYORS (C) CARRY THE PAYMENT UP TO THE MACHINE SUPERVISOR (D). IF CHANGE IS REQUIRED HE WILL PLACE IT IN THE CHUTE (E) FROM WHENCE IT WILL PASS DOWN THE HOLLOW BEARD OF THE SPHINX (F) AND OUT AT (G). THE SUPERVISOR (D) THEN OPERATES THE FOOT PEDAL (H) AND RELEASES THE PIVOTED WEIGHING ARM (J). THE WEIGHT OF THE CUSTOMER WORKS AGAINST MASSIVE COIL SPRINGS (K). BY WAY OF THE GEARS (L) THE WEIGHING ARM RAISES THE BAR (M) AND CONSEQUENTLY DRAWS DOWN THE ROD (N) THE ELECTRIC CONTACT (O) ON THIS ROD STOPS IN TOUCH WITH ONE OF THE SIXTY ELECTRIC CONTACTS (P), EACH OF WHICH OPERATES A DIFFERENT PHONOGRAPH (Q) SPEAKING A DIFFERENT WEIGHT. WHERE THE ELECTRIC CONTACT (O) STOPS IS GOVERNED BY THE WEIGHT OF THE PERSON ON THE WEIGHING PLATFORM. AS WELL AS OPERATING ONE OF THE PHONOGRAPHS, THE CONTACT ALSO STARTS THE MOTOR (R) DRIVING THE MOUTH MECHANISM (S) AND THE EYELIDS (T). THUS THE SPHINX REALISTICALLY OPENS ITS MOUTH AND

BLINKS ITS EYES AS IT SPEAKS. POWER FOR THE ELECTRIC CIRCUITRY COMES FROM A GENERATOR (U) DRIVEN BY A SMALL STEAM ENGINE (V). THIS IN TURN IS POWERED BY FOUR BOILERS (W) MOUNTED IN THE CENTRES OF ADJUSTABLE CONCAVE MIRRORS (X) WHICH USE THE HOT EGYPTIAN SUN TO BOIL THE WATER. THE STEAM PASSES THROUGH FLEXIBLE TUBES (Y) TO THE ENGINE. SHOULD THE CUSTOMER WISH TO SUBTRACT THE WEIGHT OF CAMELS, LUGGAGE OR CLOTHES, THE 'ABACUS CALCULATOR' OR FRAME OF SLIDING BEADS (Z) CAN BE USED. AS WELL AS THE SPOKEN WEIGHT, A LARGE DIAL ON THE CHEST OF THE SPHINX (1) GIVES A VISUAL WEIGHT READING WITH CONVERSION FIGURES FOR ALL LANGUAGES, INCLUDING HIEROGLYPHS. THE SPHINX ALSO CONTAINS A GALLERY OF EGYPTIAN ASTROLOGY, WHERE ONE MAY, WITH THE HELP OF THE HEAVENLY BODIES, SEE INTO ONE'S FUTURE (2), AND THE GASTRONOMIC DELIGHTS OF THE 'GIZA BREAK' RESTAURANT MAY BE ENJOYED AS A FITTING CLIMAX TO THE DAY'S TRIP (3).

BLACKPOOL TOWER

THE NORMAL WICK.

NORMAL STRING CANDLE WICK — CANDLE REQUIRING TRIMMING

THE NORMAL CANDLE WICK IS A TIGHTLY SPIRALLED STRING AND REQUIRES REGULAR AND CAREFUL TRIMMING TO PREVENT IT GIVING OFF SMOKE AND FUMES (RIGHT).

BALMORAL CASTLE, SCOTLAND: FITTED WITH A GIANT MULTI-WICK TO ILLUMINATE COURTYARDS AT NIGHT.

THE BLACKPOOL TOWER CANDLE MANUFACTURY ~ 1900.

HOW THE CANDLES ARE MADE.

POSITION OF ARMS WHEN LOWERING COMPLETE CANDLES

WINCH ROOM

CANDLE ROPE

LIFT

TANKS IN WHICH GIANT MULTI-WICK CANDLES ARE MADE

TUBES IN WHICH CANDLES ARE FORMED

COMPLETED CANDLES ARE LOWERED DOWN THESE CHUTES WHILE STILL FLEXIBLE

CUTTING AND PACKING BUILDING

BOILER — FURNACES

THE CANDLE ROPE RAISES AND LOWERS THE WICK IN THE FORMING TUBE OF HOT MOLTEN WAX UNTIL A COATING OF THE REQUIRED THICKNESS IS FORMED. IT IS THEN LOWERED TO THE CUTTING BUILDING.

COPPERTHWAITE'S GIANT MULTI-WICK RESTAURANT.

SOFT LIGHT — AND WARMTH

HOT-PLATES

SECTION THROUGH CANDLE

GUIDES

WEIGHTS

A BRASS LIP AROUND THE INSIDE EDGE OF THE TABLE HOLDS THE GIANT MULTI-WICK CANDLE IN POSITION, WHILE THE WEIGHTS RAISE IT AS IT BURNS. THE RESTAURANT IS CONSTRUCTED ON A HIGH IRON FRAMEWORK TO ALLOW FOR EASY REPLACEMENT OF THE CANDLES.

COPPERTHWAITE'S HEATED WATER CLOSET IN WHICH CANDLES WARM THE SEAT AND PREVENT FREEZING IN WINTER.

RUBBER COATED THIN IRON SEAT

IRON CASING (REMOVABLE)

CANDLES

THE END IS NIGH!

THE 'ILLUMINARY STRIP.'

WICKS

GLASS WIND SHIELDS

WOOD BASE

CONTINUOUS CANDLE

THE ORIGINAL INSPIRATION FOR THE BLACKPOOL ILLUMINATIONS.

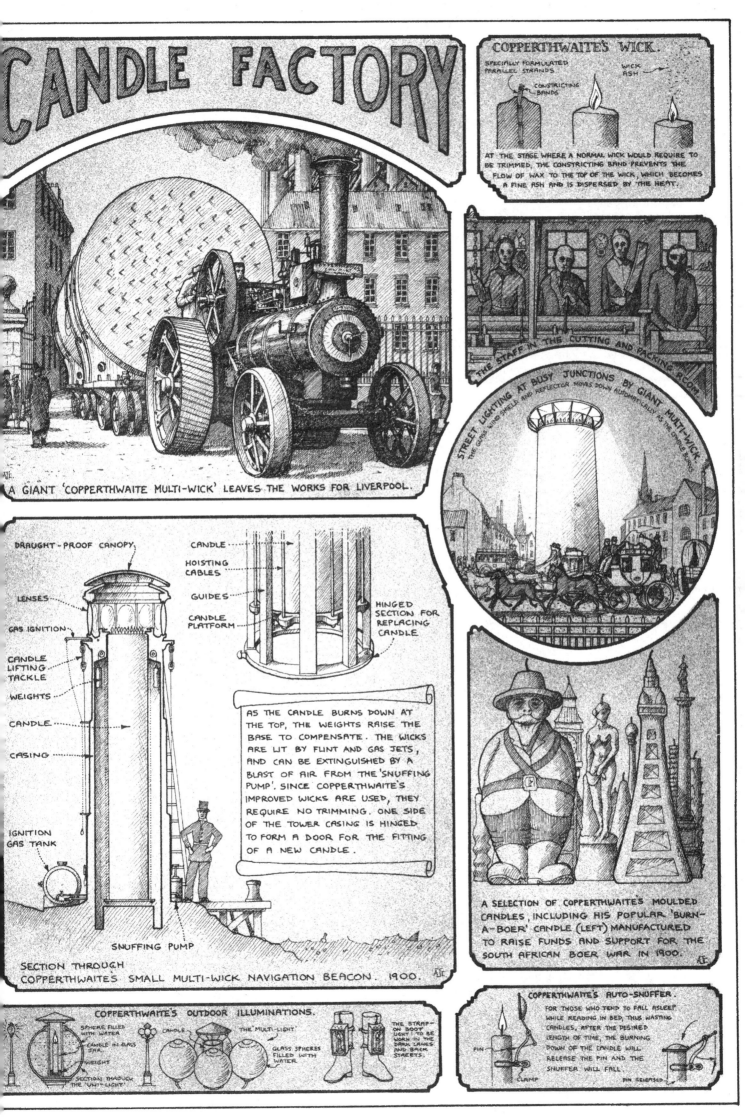

CANDLE FACTORY

A GIANT 'COPPERTHWAITE MULTI-WICK' LEAVES THE WORKS FOR LIVERPOOL.

COPPERTHWAITE'S WICK.

SPECIALLY FORMULATED PARALLEL STRANDS

WICK ASH

CONSTRICTING BANDS

AT THE STAGE WHERE A NORMAL WICK WOULD REQUIRE TO BE TRIMMED, THE CONSTRICTING BAND PREVENTS THE FLOW OF WAX TO THE TOP OF THE WICK, WHICH BECOMES A FINE ASH AND IS DISPERSED BY THE HEAT.

THE STAFF IN THE CUTTING AND PACKING ROOM.

STREET LIGHTING AT BUSY JUNCTIONS BY GIANT MULTI-WICK. THE GLASS WIND SHIELD AND REFLECTOR MOVES DOWN AUTOMATICALLY AS THE CANDLE BURNS.

DRAUGHT-PROOF CANOPY.

LENSES

GAS IGNITION

CANDLE LIFTING TACKLE

WEIGHTS

CANDLE

CASING

IGNITION GAS TANK

CANDLE

HOISTING CABLES

GUIDES

CANDLE PLATFORM

HINGED SECTION FOR REPLACING CANDLE

AS THE CANDLE BURNS DOWN AT THE TOP, THE WEIGHTS RAISE THE BASE TO COMPENSATE. THE WICKS ARE LIT BY FLINT AND GAS JETS, AND CAN BE EXTINGUISHED BY A BLAST OF AIR FROM THE 'SNUFFING PUMP'. SINCE COPPERTHWAITE'S IMPROVED WICKS ARE USED, THEY REQUIRE NO TRIMMING. ONE SIDE OF THE TOWER CASING IS HINGED TO FORM A DOOR FOR THE FITTING OF A NEW CANDLE.

SNUFFING PUMP

SECTION THROUGH
COPPERTHWAITES SMALL MULTI-WICK NAVIGATION BEACON. 1900.

A SELECTION OF COPPERTHWAITES MOULDED CANDLES, INCLUDING HIS POPULAR 'BURN-A-BOER' CANDLE (LEFT) MANUFACTURED TO RAISE FUNDS AND SUPPORT FOR THE SOUTH AFRICAN BOER WAR IN 1900.

COPPERTHWAITE'S OUTDOOR ILLUMINATIONS.

SPHERE FILLED WITH WATER

CANDLE IN GLASS JAR

WEIGHT

SECTION THROUGH THE 'UNI'-LIGHT

CANDLE

THE 'MULTI-LIGHT'

GLASS SPHERES FILLED WITH WATER

THE 'STRAP-ON BOOT-LIGHT' TO BE WORN IN THE DARK LANES AND BACK STREETS.

COPPERTHWAITE'S AUTO-SNUFFER.

FOR THOSE WHO TEND TO FALL ASLEEP WHILE READING IN BED, THUS WASTING CANDLES, AFTER THE DESIRED LENGTH OF TIME, THE BURNING DOWN OF THE CANDLE WILL RELEASE THE PIN AND THE SNUFFER WILL FALL.

PIN

CLAMP

PIN RELEASED

BLACKPOOL TOWER CANDLE MANUFACTURY 1899-1900

As an 'improver' to existing structures, Copperthwaite's development of Blackpool Tower is famous to this day and currently commemorated in the Memory Lane exhibition at the Tower.

Originally conceived as a landmark in the flat Lancashire landscape, the original Tower was inspired by the Eiffel Tower in Paris which, in turn, was derided by visiting Blackpool Councillors as 'ideal' except – 'there's nowt at t'bottom to tek brass'. Requested by local entrepreneurs to add another 'profit centre' to the Tower without spoiling its proven internal 'brass-taking' attractions, Copperthwaite advocated the idea of a candle manufactury with the slogan 'All's Right with Light'.

This was constructed in record time and proved an immediate financial success and yet another popular tourist attraction in the seaside town. A motion by the opposition party in the Town Council to officially change 'Blackpool Tower' to 'Blackpool Stick' was, however, narrowly defeated.

A great many new jobs were created especially 'out of season'. Blackpool Rock workers were recruited to use their experience and cut and pack candles in the specially designed buildings at the foot of the Tower and many added saucy messages to the packing.

As the pages for the Professor's scrapbook show there were many and varied commercial off-shoots of the candle venture all designed to bring a sparkle to the eye of any enterprising Lancashire businessman.

The Copperthwaite Patent *Heated Water Closet* found instant fashionable favour in the little rooms of the rich and famous. The Candle Company records sales of single, double and even triple seaters to many town and country mansions. A mobile example is thought to still exist in a Royal Tram exhibited at the National Railway Museum and Queen Victoria is on record as finding it 'engaging'.

The novelty candle business survives today but examples are usually on a considerably smaller scale than Copperthwaite's flaming epics – his Burn-a-Boer 30-Day Burner was some thirty feet high.

His giant *'Multi-Wick'* candles enjoyed commercial success in a wide variety of guises – businessmen and local authorities quickly finding a ready application for steady, inexpensive heat and light. Special restaurants opened with tables designed around multi-wicks; navigation beacons were installed and tested by Trinity House on hazards from Wick to Holy Island; multi-coloured multi-wicks installed in Shaftesbury Avenue and Drury Lane threatened to bring London's transport and sewage system to a standstill with progressively growing floods of molten wax.

Even in Victorian invention-conscious society such developments as the *Strap-on Boot Light* did not enjoy universal acclaim, although the Grand lodge of Scotland records a motion to incorporate their use into a secret Masonic ritual. The painful experience of a Grand Worshipable Master's ceremonial apron actually catching fire during an initiation finally extinguished the suggestion. He is officially recorded in the minutes as shouting 'That's 'snuff of them!'

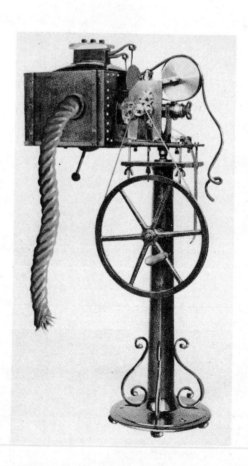

Copperthwaite's Patent 'Wickmaster', a machine designed and constructed to convert and recycle old rope into new candle wicks. This is the machine which inspired the expression 'Money For Old Rope'.

ST PAUL'S CATHEDRAL ROTA-DOME 1900-1902

A portrait of Queen Victoria holding her personal copy of the plans for the St Paul's Rota-Dome and Roof Garden. St Paul's with its controversial new spinning mitres can be clearly seen in the background.

In December of 1900 Professor Copperthwaite attended a service at St Paul's Cathedral to celebrate 'the beginning of a new and peaceful century'.

After the service Copperthwaite wandered through the Cathedral, admiring the scale of the building and the beauty of its design. The dome in particular fascinated him, although with his naturally mechanical mind he felt it should actually do something rather than just be a simple dome. A small, rather tired-looking gentleman engaged him in conversation for some time, and it was only as their meeting ended that Copperthwaite discovered his companion was the cathedral organist. He evidently complained to Copperthwaite that the task of playing the organ for long periods during special services could be quite exhausting, and it was becoming more and more difficult to find individuals with the skill and strength to play the huge instrument.

Almost immediately Copperthwaite's mechanically orientated mind came up with a plan. He would design a dome for the Cathedral that would rotate under the 'free power of the Heavenly winds', and this would operate the organ mechanically. This principle had been used frequently on small organ clocks – all he had to do was to scale the mechanism up and adapt it to work powered by the rotating dome. The Primate of All-England, The Archbishop of Canterbury, quickly approved Copperthwaite's plan and the Professor spent the next two years on the task of re-building the dome. The mechanism to turn the Dome still exists intact to this day but its use is restricted by modern Building Regulations and the Health and Safety at Work Act.

The Professor also commissioned a model St Paul's which was, in fact, a complete clock, with the dome rotating on the hour to work miniature organ and bellows. A series of pin drums provided various tunes.

The Roof Gardens were a typical Copperthwaite embellishment and were designed to bring home 'the wonders of God's natural creation to the humble worshipper' and provide 'an English home for the diverse plants catalogued in the Good Book'. These gardens became a popular promenade for Society and the first home for many rare species of flora brought home from pilgrimages to the Holy Land and other religious centres.

The 'Tomb of the Unknown Architect' is thought to be a joke on Copperthwaite's part as a heavy-handed comment on the work he had undertaken – without fee – for St Paul's Cathedral.

'This man Napoleon is no hero. I have never seen him except on horseback. I believe he is a very frightened man, unable to get off of a very brave horse.'
Private Letters; AJC, 1839

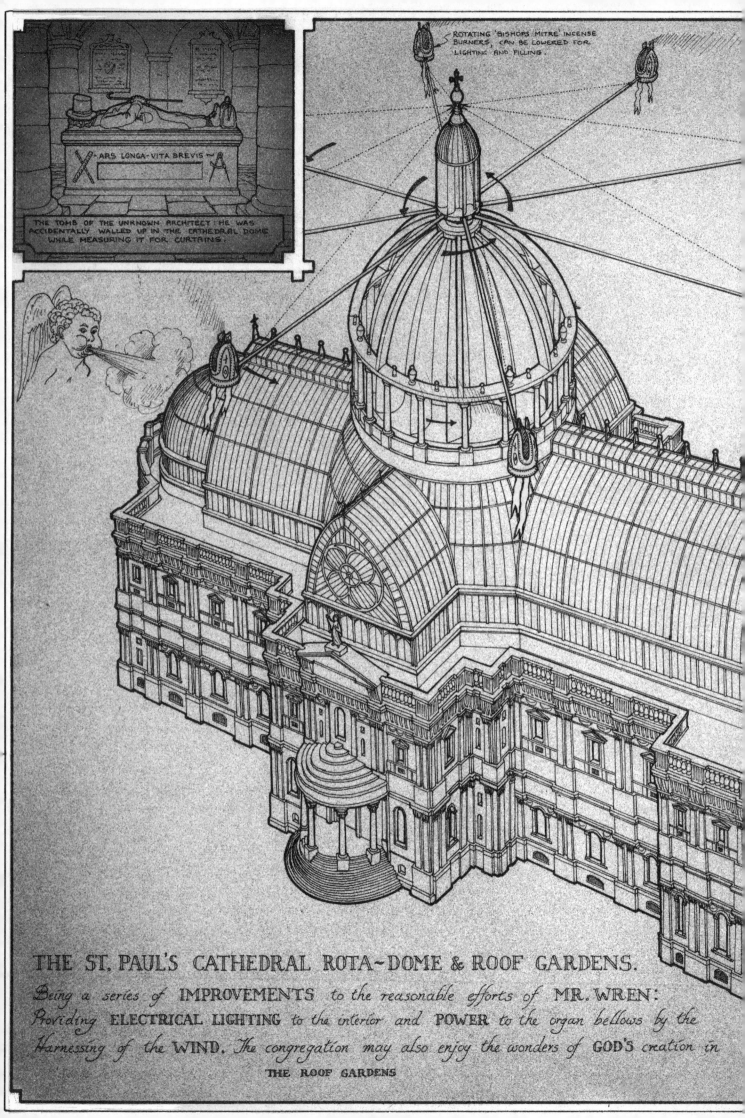

ROTATING 'BISHOPS MITRE' INCENSE
BURNERS, CAN BE LOWERED FOR
LIGHTING AND FILLING.

THE TOMB OF THE UNKNOWN ARCHITECT : HE WAS
ACCIDENTALLY WALLED UP IN THE CATHEDRAL DOME
WHILE MEASURING IT FOR CURTAINS.

ARS LONGA · VITA BREVIS

THE ST. PAUL'S CATHEDRAL ROTA~DOME & ROOF GARDENS.

Being a series of IMPROVEMENTS to the reasonable efforts of MR. WREN:
Providing ELECTRICAL LIGHTING to the interior and POWER to the organ bellows by the
Harnessing of the WIND. The congregation may also enjoy the wonders of GOD'S creation in

THE ROOF GARDENS

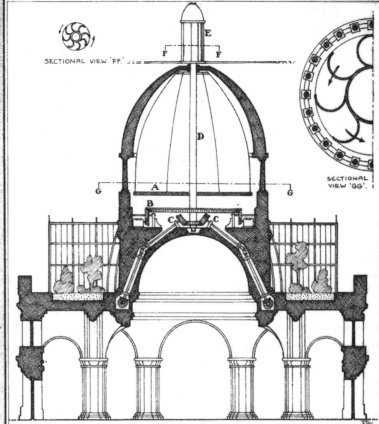

THE OLD CATHEDRAL ORGANIST (WITH HEARING AID DUE TO DEAFNESS (CAUSED BY LOW NOTES) IN FRONT OF ONE OF THE FOUR SETS OF WIND-POWERED BELLOWS.

SECTIONAL VIEW 'FF.'

SECTIONAL VIEW 'GG'.

A SECTIONAL VIEW THROUGH THE ROTA-DOME, SHOWING:
THE WIND POWERED TURBINE REPLACING THE EXISTING DOME (A). THIS IS MOUNTED ON THE ROTATING VERTICAL SHAFT (D), AS IS THE STARTER TURBINE. (E). THE GEARS (B) DRIVE THE ELECTRIC GENERATORS TO PROVIDE LIGHTING IN THE CATHEDRAL, WHILE THE GEARS (C) DRIVE THE ORGAN BELLOWS BY WAY OF LONG CONNECTING RODS.

A.F.Fopperthwaite

ST. PAUL'S CATHEDRAL
ROOF GARDENS.

CONSIDER THE LILIES OF THE FIELD

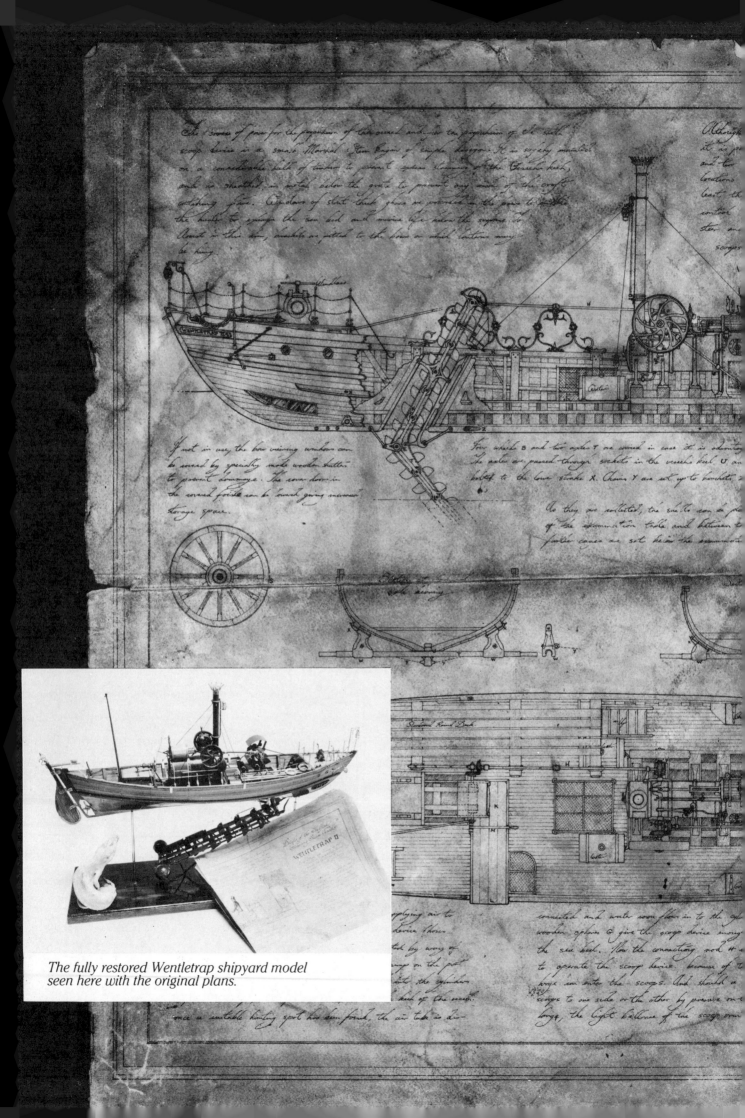

The fully restored Wentletrap shipyard model
seen here with the original plans.

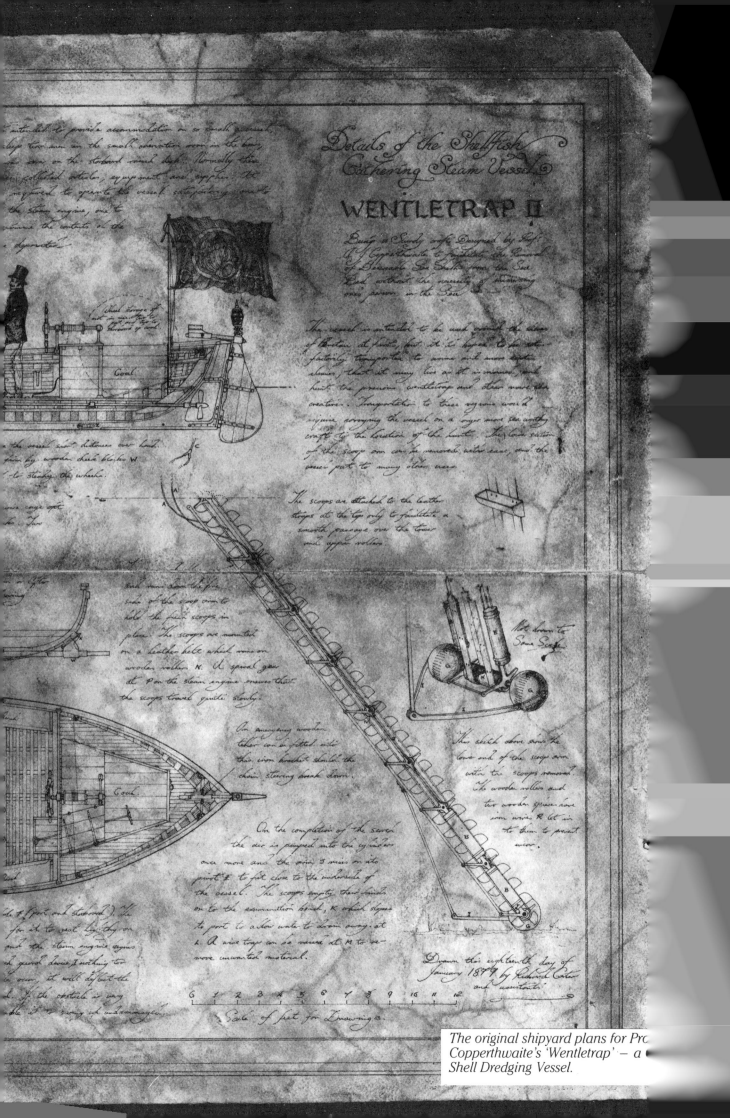

The original shipyard plans for Prof. Copperthwaite's 'Wentletrap' – a ... Shell Dredging Vessel.

THE WENTLETRAP
A Gentleman's Shell Dredging Vessel
1879

Originally conceived as a relaxation, Copperthwaite's study of the natural world quickly took on the mantle of a fixation and was pursued with the same fanatical enthusiasm that characterised his architectural improvements.

As with many Victorian gentlemen of letters, the formation of his personal Cabinet of Curios became a lifetime pre-occupation. The collecting of rare and interesting creatures from all corners of the Empire became his true love and consuming interest but his singular speciality was conchology — the collecting of shells. Even this speciality became narrowed and he spent a great many years searching for one specific species — the Precious Wentletrap.

Only two specimens had been recorded by the mid-19th century — one in the British Museum and the other in a foreign private collection. When a further superb example was offered at auction in London, Copperthwaite examined it carefully beforehand to make sure that it was not a rice-paste Chinese fake. He was, however, delayed on his way to the sale and arrived to see the shell 'knocked down' to the Danish collector Chris Hwass who already owned one! Copperthwaite was then aghast to see Hwass take his newly bought prize, drop it to the floor and crush it under his heel! He would still have the only specimen in private hands!

Copperthwaite determined at that moment to search for and find his very own Precious Wentletrap. Nothing would do for the task but his own specifically designed gentleman's dredging vessel — a ship of revolutionary design — soon to be christened 'The Wentletrap'. The original plans remain to this day and show the unmistakable draftsmanship of the master ship designer of the period — Richard Carter. The shipyard model — presented to the Professor at the launch — has also survived and serves as a potent reminder of the tenacity of this great collector. As a footnote, Copperthwaite never did record that he had found the elusive *Epitonium scalare*.

Professor A J Copperthwaite examines the shipyard model of his shell-dredging vessel, 'The Wentletrap', with his faithful mascot, Edna, the Australian Blue Tongued Skink looking on.

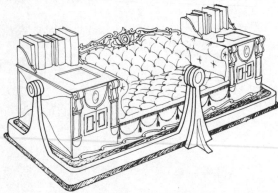

A gimbolled sofa designed by Copperthwaite for the salon in the Wentletrap.

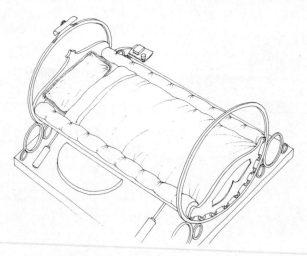

The Captain's Bed in the Wentletrap was not gimbolled but constructed within a series of castors and hoops to provide a measure of stability. The Professor's introduction of a reading light on the head-board would appear to be fairly revolutionary for the period.

THE BIG BEN NATIONAL CLOCK 1906

The 'improvement' of one of the most famous landmarks in the world was to be one of the last recorded major projects in A J Copperthwaite's illustrious career.

He records his feelings that the 'Big Ben' clock at the Palace of Westminster could be 'more truly a symbol of Empire' with the simple (to him) addition of some dramatic features.

He proposed housing four life-size lions in the casing above Westminster Tower Clock with a mechanism to propel them into view on the hour. At the same time as the appearance of the lions over London a mechanically produced roar would be emitted for each hour, just after the striking of the Big Ben bell.

Synchronised with the lions and the roar-making device the flags of the Empire would proudly unfurl down the four sides of the Tower.

The technology and machinery to produce these effects was all created and designed by Copperthwaite and installed under his personal direction. Extra staff were trained by him to ensure that everything worked on time. Copperthwaite records that it was 'most imperative that there be no misadventures with the mechanisms or engines for such a potent and public display of national pride'.

Copperthwaite was especially concerned with the appearance of the Empire flags. He insisted that they all be repaired and maintained, virtually on a daily basis. A full-time seamstress was therefore employed and accommodated at the foot of the Tower to maintain these flags and keep them flying in pristine condition. The Professor was obviously fascinated by the newly created post and his scrapbooks contain at least two detailed sketches of the flag seamstress. These also illustrate some of the special flag repair equipment which Copperthwaite designed to 'make (her) endeavours most efficient'.

The lions and roar-making device evidently remain hidden in the Tower to this day but have not been heard or seen publicly since they were banned at the outbreak of the First World War. Palace of Westminster security guards tell stories of growlings heard high up in the Tower on 'significant nights' for Britain but sceptics blame the wind!

An early sketch of The National Lion Clock (with the artist in the foreground) showing an earlier arrangement of flag display before the (later) flag-rollers were introduced.

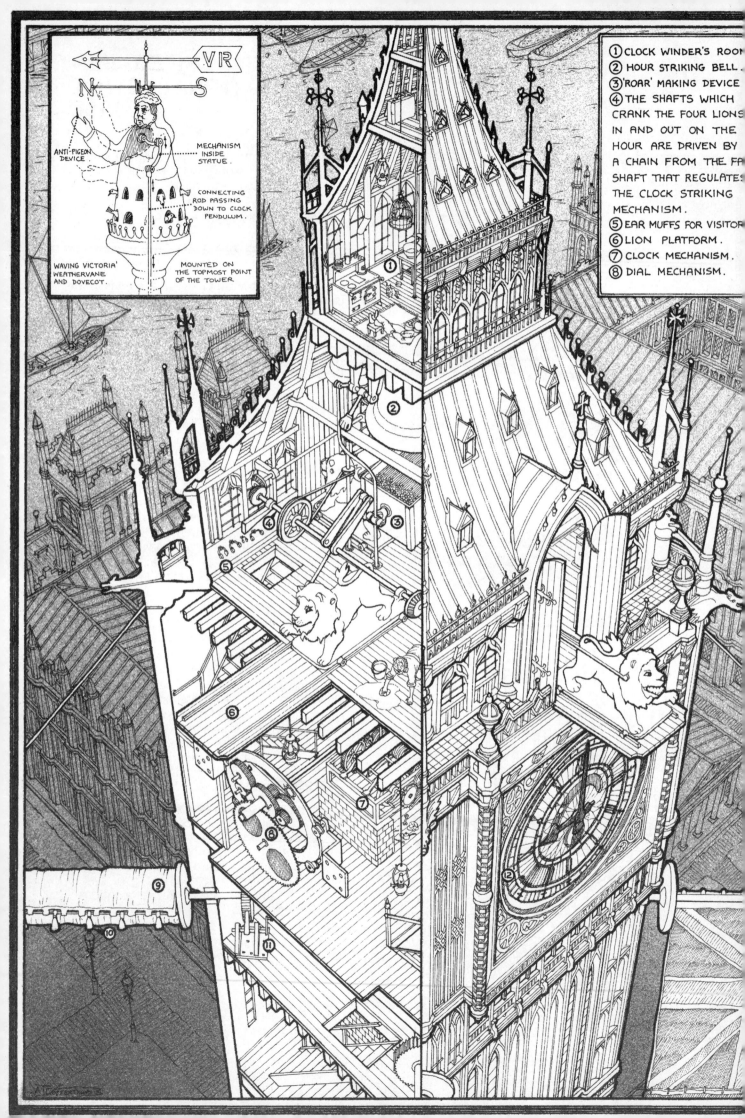

① CLOCK WINDER'S ROOM
② HOUR STRIKING BELL
③ 'ROAR' MAKING DEVICE
④ THE SHAFTS WHICH
   CRANK THE FOUR LIONS
   IN AND OUT ON THE
   HOUR ARE DRIVEN BY
   A CHAIN FROM THE FA..
   SHAFT THAT REGULATES
   THE CLOCK STRIKING
   MECHANISM.
⑤ EAR MUFFS FOR VISITOR
⑥ LION PLATFORM.
⑦ CLOCK MECHANISM.
⑧ DIAL MECHANISM.

VR

N
S

ANTI-PIGEON
DEVICE.

MECHANISM
INSIDE
STATUE.

CONNECTING
ROD PASSING
DOWN TO CLOCK
PENDULUM.

WAVING VICTORIA'
WEATHERVANE
AND DOVECOT.

MOUNTED ON
THE TOPMOST POINT
OF THE TOWER

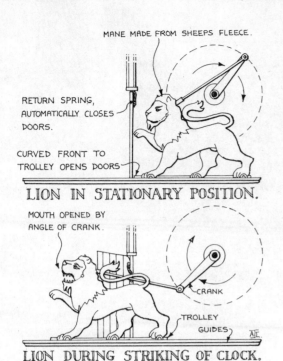

MANE MADE FROM SHEEPS FLEECE.

RETURN SPRING, AUTOMATICALLY CLOSES DOORS.

CURVED FRONT TO TROLLEY OPENS DOORS.

LION IN STATIONARY POSITION.

MOUTH OPENED BY ANGLE OF CRANK.

CRANK

TROLLEY GUIDES

LION DURING STRIKING OF CLOCK.

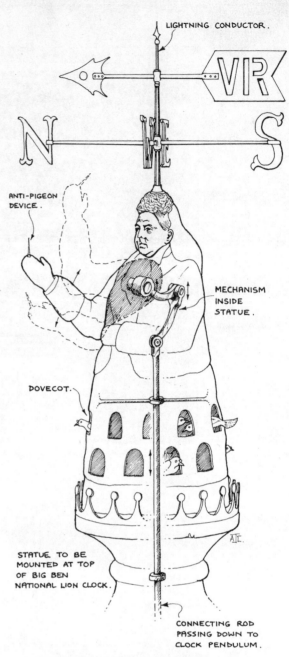

LIGHTNING CONDUCTOR.

VR

N · S

ANTI-PIGEON DEVICE.

MECHANISM INSIDE STATUE.

DOVECOT.

STATUE TO BE MOUNTED AT TOP OF BIG BEN NATIONAL LION CLOCK.

CONNECTING ROD PASSING DOWN TO CLOCK PENDULUM.

'WAVING VICTORIA' WEATHER VANE AND DOVECOT.

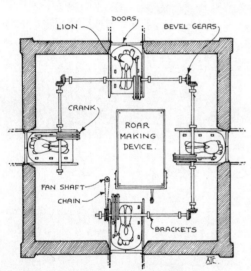

LION   DOORS   BEVEL GEARS

CRANK

ROAR MAKING DEVICE.

FAN SHAFT

CHAIN

BRACKETS

HOW THE FOUR LIONS ARE OPERATED.

Key to the cut-away drawing:-

When the clock mechanism (20) strikes the hour, the fan (17) which controls the speed of the hour-striking mechanism rotates quickly on the shaft (19), driving the chain drive (15) that cranks the four lions (14) in and out through their spring-loaded doors (1). At the same time the cable (18) which rises and falls to strike the hours on Big Ben (9) rocks an iron box (16) up and down, and produces the lion's roar by means of iron balls rolling back and forth on tin trays (visible in the cut-away section). As the hour-striking mechanism runs, it operates a chain drive (21) to the shaft on which the flag-raising cables are wound (22). The flag-staffs (6) are raised by the cables (4) winding on to the drums (22). The flags automatically unfurl as the furlong ropes become slack (5). At one minute past the hour the chain and mechanism (21) automatically disengage, and the flagstaffs are drawn down by counterbalance weights into their furled position until the next hour.

The pendulum of the clock (11) which swings in the weight chamber (23) also operates the 'Waving Victoria Windvane' on the very top of the tower by means of the connecting rod (10).

Visitors to the tower can protect their ears against the volume of the bells by hiring ear-muffs at the information stand (27).

The Clock Room also contains the dial-cleaning equipment (25) and lighting facilities for the dial by night (26). The clock-winder and lamp-lighter has a rest room (24) built into the remaining available space. The dials themselves have been improved by the addition of a moon phase disc (3) showing the age of the moon, and a solar disc (2) giving the position of the sun at any time during the day. To prevent any inaccuracies in the operation of this informative mechanism, a large tank of clock oil (12) is housed in the bell chamber.

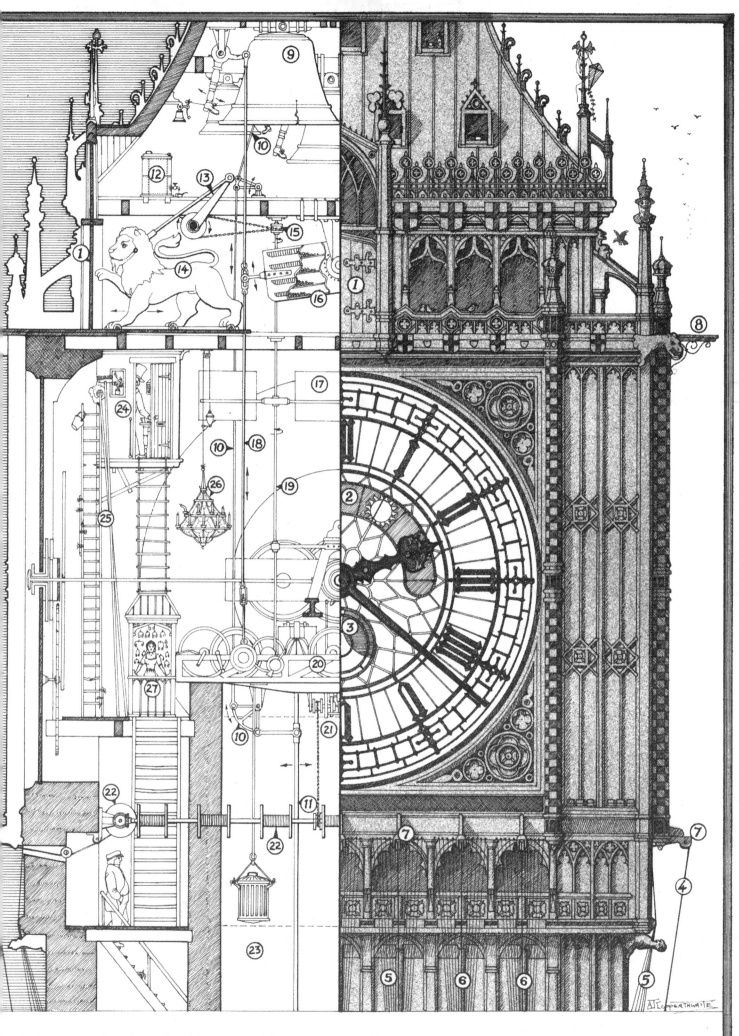

ne detailed drawings from Copperthwaite's 1st National Clock presentation to The Palace of Westminster Sub-
mittee for The Fabric.

Bibliography,
Research Sources,
Further Reading, etc.

Feathered Fancier (periodical), Vol. 3 No. 7 (1885), An appeal for the replacement of the humble Canary with a more robust species in British Mines. (signed *AJC*) (Copperthwaite advocated the training of talking Indian Mynah Birds to shout warnings of dangerous gas. Ed.)

The British Conchology Journal (182 Vol. 15. Nos. 8 and 9), The Search for the Precious Wentletrap *(Epitonium scalare)* – being an account of the further voyages of 'The Wentletrap'. Copperthwaite & de Burgh.

Lloyds Shipping Gazette (periodical), June, 1898 'The opening of the Tower Bridge Boatwash and the unfortunate error which occasioned the early retiral of the Official Opening Party.'

House of Commons Green and White Papers, Hansard (various dates).

Proceedings of the Welsh Office Proposals for the change-of-use from 'a Castle to a Carp Farm', Cardiff. 1874.

Musicians Union Report of the Annual General Meeting, 1897. Formation of deputation to protest against the Fully Automatic Steam-Powered Orchestra at the Albert Hall. Day of National Discord proposed.

The Times, Court Circular, 1st August, 1897.'The first Garden Party to require the new Inflatable State Marquee'. . . by the Hon. Nigel Dempster.

The Trough or Gentleman's Caterer (trade periodical), September, 1881. 'Disquiet on the Thames as new revolving Restaurant opens – are we being taken for a ride?' asks 'Gourmet'.

The Pondkeeper and Fancy Fish Fanatic, No. 445, 1878. 'Report on the breeding activities of *Carpus copperthwaittii* at Caernarvon' (A Voyeur).

Catering Circular (specialist trade publication), 1881 – September/October.'Revolving restaurants – a revolution in catering?' (editorial).

The Herbalist – (several issues during 1837-40), field trials of new Copperthwaite varieties currently under cultivation at Glastonbury – magical powers claimed.

War Department Memos (various) (1) (WWR/453/45a) Feasibility study on Stonehenge Warning System and the proposals of Professor A J Copperthwaite; (2) (WWR/554/54a,b) Buckingham Palace Inflatable Marquee – potential use as Officer's Mess in battle – a study; (3) (WWD/333/564c)Egyptian Sector Intelligence Report 'The Speaking Sphinx – what else could it say?'

Lloyds Shipping Gazette No. 3432 (1899),'The London Boatwash – a new found pride in the line'. No. 3441 (1900), 'Suds from Boatwash a Hazard to Shipping' (letter from Pilot).

Trinity House Report (news item) No. 3, 1886, 'Use of Eddystone in commercial fishing venture'.

The Yorkshire Horologist, 1907 (Winter),Whitby chapter visit Big Ben Lion Clock – members' views – *Mainspring* suggests 'Make **Your** Mantle Clock Roar'.

Punch (1900-1907), various cartoons, etc. on St Paul's Rota-Dome, and Big Ben National Lion Clock. 'Prince Albert up in arms', 'High Church turns full circle', etc.

The Chanter (Journal of the Bagpipe Appreciation Society), Spring, 1882. 'Proposed Edinburgh Castle School – hailed as major shot under the arm for aspiring pipers'.

Scottish Civil Engineer – Annual Report, 1889. 'Concern over safety of Forth Railway Bridge if converted to whisky store – stress, weight involved, etc.')

(Editor's note: These concerns were confirmed as being fully justified by the ScotRail (S.E.Area) Area Civil Engineer in 1986. 'The main tubes of the Bridge vary from about 12ft diameter to some 6.5ft and if you calculate the volume of these and multiply by the weight of liquid which could be contained . . . the structure would certainly collapse').

'If I were honest, I would say no, I do not like civilisation. It isolates us from Nature. Civilisation is planting grass to keep people off.'
Letter to Prince Albert; AJC, 1859

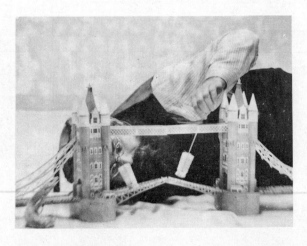

A rare informal photograph of Professor Copperthwaite at work on an early Tower Bridge Boat-Wash model.